W. R. King

Experimental and theoretical investigations of materalis for defensive amor

W. R. King

Experimental and theoretical investigations of materalis for defensive amor

ISBN/EAN: 9783742862563

Manufactured in Europe, USA, Canada, Australia, Japa

Cover: Foto ©Andreas Hilbeck / pixelio.de

Manufactured and distributed by brebook publishing software
(www.brebook.com)

W. R. King

Experimental and theoretical investigations of materalis for defensive amor

Gun Pendulum

Weight of gun alone	[illegible]	Diameter of shot	one inch
[illegible]	[illegible]	Length of equivalent simple pendulum	[illegible]
[illegible]	[illegible]		
[illegible]	[illegible]	Time of vibration	2 seconds

PROFESSIONAL PAPERS, CORPS OF ENGINEERS, U.S. ARMY.
No. 17.

REPORT

ON CERTAIN

EXPERIMENTAL AND THEORETICAL INVESTIGATIONS

RELATIVE TO THE

QUALITY, FORM, AND COMBINATION

OF

MATERIALS FOR DEFENSIVE ARMOR.

TOGETHER WITH

INCIDENTAL FACTS RELATIVE TO THEIR USE

FOR

INDUSTRIAL PURPOSES.

MADE BY DIRECTION OF

BVT. MAJ. GEN'L A. A. HUMPHREYS,
BRIG. GEN'L AND CHIEF OF ENGINEERS, U. S. A.

BY

BVT. MAJ. W. R. KING,
CAPT. OF ENGINEERS, U. S. A.

WASHINGTON:
GOVERNMENT PRINTING OFFICE.
1870.

INDEX.

Subject.	Page.	Figure.	Plate.
Letter	3		
Introduction	5		
Description of apparatus	9		
Gun	9		(Frontispiece)
Projectiles	9	All.	III
Powder	10		
Target-frame	10	1, 2	I
Ballistic pendulum	11		
Testing machine	12		
Indicator	12	1	II
Planimeter	13		
Whirling machine	13		
Sand-box	14	2	I
Indenting tools—cutter	15	3, 4, 5	XXVII
Impact of projectiles	16		
Penetration	19	1	XXI
(a) General theory of penetration	19		
(b) Formula for perforation	24	1, 2, 3, 4	XXI
(c) Deduction of new formula	**26**	**1, 2, 3, 4**	**XXI, XXII, XXIII**
Concussion	31		
Effect of concussion on structure of metal	33	2, 3	XXIV
Oblique impact	39	5, 6, 7	XIX, XX, XXI
Quality of metal for armor-plating	45	3, 4, 5, 6	I, II, XXIV
Economy of plating	59		
Solid plating	60		VI, VII
Laminated plating	62		VIII, IX, X
Separated plates	67		XI
Plates separated by bars of lead	**68**		**[1]XII**
Beam, or girder, target	69	1, 2, 3	XIII
Tubular target	70		XII
Perforated or cellular plates	70		XI
Puddled iron	71		XIII
Annealed iron	72		VIII
Chilled iron	73		XIV
Lead concrete	74		XVII, XVIII

[1] Bottom, front, and back.

Subject.	Page.	Figure.	Plate.
Sand between iron plates	76		
Penetration in sand	77	8	XIII
Steel	81		
Different processes	81-85		
1st. Common	81		
2nd. Bessemer	82		XV, XVI
3rd. Richardson's	82		
4th. Martin's	83		
5th. Uchatius's	83		
6th. Shower	83		
7th. Nitrate	83		
8th. Siemens'	84		
9th. Mellodie & Company's	84		
10th. Chenot's	84		
11th. Smith's	84		
12th. Heaton's	84		
13th. Ojers'	85		
14th. Radcliff's	85		
15th. Ellershausen's	85		
16th. Berard's	85		
Compared with iron	86		
Bolts	89		XXV, XXVI
Strains upon bolts	90		
Different kinds of bolts	91		
Form and size of thread	93	3, 4, 5, 6	XXV
Depth and thickness of nut	95	4	XXIV
Projectiles	99		IV, V, XXII
Pointed vs. flat-headed shot	101		
Possible improvements in projectiles	104		

WASHINGTON, D. C., *April* 21, 1870.

BVT. MAJ. GEN. A. A. HUMPHREYS,

Brig. Gen. and Chief of Engineers U. S. A.

GENERAL: I have the honor to submit the following report on a series of experiments and theoretical investigations relative to the use of armor-plating in connection with land defenses.

This report was originally intended to include only an account of the experiments on a reduced scale, which have by your direction constituted a portion of my duties at this office, and of which the partial results have been reported from time to time.

Having had occasion, however, in comparing and verifying results obtained, to give some attention to the results of other and more extensive experiments, as well as to investigate various theories involved, some conclusions were arrived at which are thought to be of interest in connection with the direct results of these experiments, and they are therefore included.

Since diagrams and illustrations are readily understood without detailed explanations, it was not thought necessary to give a minute account of every experiment made, but merely a few illustrated examples of each class of experiments; the data not represented in the illustrations being placed in tables opposite the plates to which they belong.

Although considerable time has elapsed since these experiments were commenced, owing to delay in preparing machinery and apparatus and to other causes, they are still incomplete in many respects; some branches of the subject being omitted entirely, while others are left in doubt for want of sufficient experimental data. A complete solution to the question of armor-plating would involve the whole subject of strength and durability of materials, the various phenomena relating to the impact of bodies and the science of gunnery, as well as much of metallurgy and of mechanical engineering; and the various branches of the subject are so interwoven and mutually dependent as to be practically endless. In fact, almost every experiment made suggests a number of others, and, so far as present indications are an index to the future, this may continue indefinitely.

In view of these facts I feel no reluctance in admitting the incompleteness of this report.

Very respectfully, your obedient servant,

W. R. KING,

Captain of Engineers, Brevet Maj. U. S. A.

INTRODUCTION.

The question is often asked, "Can anything relative to armor-plating deduced from experiments with small projectiles and targets be relied upon as applicable to large ones?"—a question which suggests an immediate explanation of the nature and object of the experiments upon which this report is based.

It should be stated in the outset that these experiments were not intended as an entire substitute for large ones, but that they were undertaken as auxiliaries or finders, with a view to ascertaining and diminishing the number and extent of the larger experiments required.

It is well known that certain points in regard to the application of metals to the purposes of armor-plating, can only be satisfactorily determined by direct experiments with the identical guns and projectiles, and materials and form of structure to be employed in service; and in fact, that *absolute certainty* of results in any case can only be attained in that way. At the same time it is equally evident that the literal carrying out of this method would involve a more extensive series of experiments than any government would be likely to undertake, and one which in point of time, would probably outlast the present generation.

In the only experiments known to have been made which could be considered as representing the exact state of things in practice, the guns were mounted on land instead of on shipboard, and they were not the guns or projectiles used by any government likely to attempt the destruction of the work experimented upon. In the elaborate experiments made in Europe, which have cost millions of dollars, I can call to mind no single instance where numerous circumstances were not approximated to or assumed, and where there were not many points of absolute difference between the experimental structures and those to be built for service; some of the points of difference being in favor of the shield and some against it.

To exemplify, we may refer to a few of the circumstances attending some of the more important experiments which have been made.

1st. By far the larger number of all the experiments of which we have record were made upon targets small in area although representing the entire thickness of parts to be used in practice; these small targets being held and braced up in various ways, generally different from the manner in which the same targets would be supported were they to form integral parts of a permanent work. This objection applies even to the experiments made upon the Gibraltar, Plymouth, Millwall, and War Office shields, at Shoeburyness, as well as to most of the experiments made in this country. In some of these cases, as, for example, the War Office shield, the exposed surface was made up of patch-work: a few square feet, only, of a given thickness or construction, so that in case any portion had given satisfactory results, it would not have necessarily followed that a whole shield of the same kind would have done as well. Again, even where whole casemates have been built, they were in no case supported by collateral and similar structures, which would be the case in practice, and which would add much to the stability of the parts experimented upon.

2nd. The masonry, especially concrete, of the experimental structures was not generally allowed sufficient time to set and become as substantial as that in the actual fortification. In fact, heavy masses of good concrete will improve in quality year after year, and for a much longer time than can be waited for for experimental purposes.

3rd. The tests applied to these structures were not, as a rule, correct imitations of what they would probably receive in service. Nearly all armor-plated forts are intended to withstand only the fire from floating batteries: these batteries, of course, being those of some power other than that erecting the defenses, and the firing to be done under the excitement of actual engagement. The experimental targets were generally fired at deliberately, from land batteries, the guns and projectiles being, with few exceptions, those of the same country as the targets; and some shields designed for elevated sites were fired at from the same level.

4th. One other point, which, though not intimately connected with the present discussion, has an important bearing upon the general question of armor plating, is the effect of concussion upon the occupants of the casemate. This question, though of vital importance, seems to have been entirely overlooked in all experiments heretofore made, and only to have been developed by the necessities of actual service. When we consider the inconvenience caused by the impact of 10-inch, and smaller shot striking upon our monitor turrets, and the fact that the concussion of one 15-inch shot would be about equal to that produced by five 10-inch shot striking at once, not to speak of the 20-inch, which would be approximately represented by sixteen 10-inch ones, it appears that there is more reason to doubt the practicability of guarding against the effect of concussion than of perforation.

These points are not mentioned as criticisms upon the manner in which the larger experiments have been made, but simply to show the impracticability of arriving at absolute certainty in this line of investigation, by making the experiments on a scale equal to that adopted for service, and to suggest the propriety of looking in some other direction for a solution to at least a portion of the numerous questions involved. It may be added that these same objections, and others equally valid, may be urged against small experiments, provided their object was to arrive at the desired result by the simple trial of small models of the various structures supposed to be suitable for the purpose. If, however, the object is to study the subject by investigating the elements, principles, and laws involved, the case assumes a different aspect.

That there *is* a law connecting the results of large and small experiments cannot reasonably be doubted, when we consider that by constructing a series of guns and corresponding targets, increasing by uniform but almost inappreciable increments from the smallest musket to the largest cannon, the results obtained by firing each gun at its corresponding target would undoubtedly form an equally continuous series, the law of which would constitute a connection between its extremes. Further than this, it may be stated that the deductions from these small experiments have been compared in various ways with those of large experiments, and that in no case has it been found that the small experiments gave incorrect results.

During this series of experiments the following general principles have been kept in view:

1st. Analysis should be employed in connection with experiments, to discover the elements upon which the final results depend and the relations between these elements. For example, the velocity, weight, form, and material of the shot, and the area, thickness, and the properties which go to make up the quality of the plate, are some of the elements upon which the various questions relative to armor-plating depend.

2nd. Only one element should be varied at a time, in order to avoid the complications which would arise from having two or more unknown quantities connected by an unknown or uncertain law. Thus, if the velocity of the shot and the thickness or quality of the plate be varied at the same time, it becomes a question what part each took in producing a change in the result. There must also be some accurate measure of the elements as well as of the result of the experiments with each combination.

3rd. Each experiment should be repeated a number of times, depending upon its importance, in order to obtain the most accurate mean results. As the number of different points in connection with armor-plating to be thus determined is very great, it will be seen that the number of experiments required must be correspondingly large.

4th. In employing the results thus obtained in constructing formulæ, the constants should be deduced from the results of experiments on a large scale, or at least verified by them as well as by the fundamental principles of mechanics. In testing formulæ in this manner, or in accounting for anomalous results obtained, the subjects of limits and extreme or exaggerated cases should be considered.

There is no reason why formulæ thus constructed should not be applied in constructing defensive works in the same manner as analogous formulæ are now employed in building bridges or other engineering works, a due allowance being made for a margin of safety.

While it is not asserted that these principles have been thoroughly carried out in all cases during these experiments, or that any remarkable success has been achieved by them, it is believed that whatever useful or valuable results have been attained are chiefly due to their observance.

DESCRIPTION OF APPARATUS.

GUN.—This was a small steel rifled gun, (frontispiece,) 3 inches in diameter and 21 inches long outside, and 1.01 inch in diameter and 19.5 inches long in the bore, with five grooves of uniform twist 0.02 inch deep, and of a pitch giving the shot but one turn in twenty-five feet, the object being to introduce as little rotary motion as would suffice to keep the shot from tumbling, in the short space between the muzzle of the gun and the target.

The gun was swung on a horizontal axis with knife-edge bearings, by eight No. 20 steel wires 0.035-inch in diameter, which were found amply strong to sustain the weight, although in order to limit the recoil to small arcs this weight was increased to 156½ pounds by lead bars, as shown in the frontispiece. The distance between the axes of suspension and oscillation was 13.035-feet, and the time of vibration, two seconds.

The recoil was measured by a slide upon the graduated arc, as with the ordinary gun-pendulum.

PROJECTILES.—These were, with a few exceptions, to be noted as they occur, made of cast steel and hardened to about a cold-chisel temper. They were turned to the exact diameter of one inch and a uniform weight of 3,115 grains, or 0.445 pound for all the elongated shot, and one-third of that weight for the spherical ones. These weights were fixed upon by taking the average weight of a number of spherical shot of the given diameter as the standard, and multiplying by three for the elongated shot.

The various forms of shot used in these experiments are shown on Plate III, and of those represented the first four were the only forms used for general purposes. The others were used only for testing their own relative merits.

With regard to the first two forms, the spherical, (Spher.) and the cylindro-spherical, (C. S.) no further description will be necessary than can be obtained from the plate. The third, ogival, (O. G.) is a form much used in Europe, the radius with which the head is struck being varied from one to two diameters of the shot. That represented in the plate, Fig. 3, has a radius of one diameter. Several others of twice that radius, not represented, were fired during the experiments.

The cylindrical form, (Cyl.) Fig. 4, was very generally used and needs no further description.

The form represented by Fig. 5 was devised to test several points relative to the shot itself, among which may be mentioned the advantage of the hollow form in increasing penetration, facilitating the process of hardening, and in overcoming the tendency to tumble, by throwing the center of gravity forward of the center of figure.

Fig. 6 represents an attempt to economize steel by using cast iron for the greater portion of the shot and a ring of hardened steel for the cutting edge.

Fig. 7 was made to test the effect of a cylindrical projection in front of the shot, and Fig. 8 to compare the sub-caliber principle of Stafford and others with the ordinary forms of projectiles.

In order to give the shot a slight rotary motion without complicating them with soft metal bases or other usual devices for securing that object, a thin flannel patch was used and gave satisfactory results.

POWDER.—Musket powder was used and was recommended as being from a lot which gave very uniform velocities. The charges were accurately weighed and placed in thin paper cases of a cylindrical form and of the same diameter as the shot. The usual charge was 300 grains, but charges as small as 3 grains were fired, which was found to be about the quantity required to throw a spherical shot out of the gun, while the maximum charge fired was 600 grains, or more than one-half the weight of the spherical shot.

TARGET-FRAME.—In order to secure the plates in the proper position to receive the shot they were firmly clamped to a heavy wrought-iron frame, shown in Figs. 1 and 2, Plate I.

As a general rule the plates were supported at the corners only, as shown in the figure, but in special cases they were arranged otherwise, as will be noticed elsewhere.

The weight of this frame was about 150 pounds, and during a portion of the experiments it was swung on an axis parallel to that of the gun pendulum and about ten feet in front of it, the recoil being measured by a graduated circle and the whole system being similar to that of the gun-pendulum. During the remaining portion of the experiments this frame was fixed about five feet in front of the muzzle of the gun, in which position it is shown in the frontispiece.

When the frame was swinging, its height was so adjusted with reference to the axis of the gun that the shot struck nearly at the center of percussion, and a shield with a small hole for the shot to pass through was placed in front of the gun, to diminish the effect of the blast upon the target. This effect, thus diminished, was measured by firing blank cartridges, and a proper allowance made in computing the momentum of the pendulum.

Ballistic Pendulum.—This was similar to the ordinary ballistic-pendulum and was mounted just in rear of the target-frame to catch the shot and measure its remaining velocity. The greatest sources of error found in using a ballistic pendulum in this manner were, first, the liability of the shot to be deflected from its course in passing through the plate, causing it to strike in an oblique direction with respect to the axis of suspension, and some distance from the center of percussion; and, second, of the pieces of plate being thrown against the pendulum at the same time with the shot.

Errors arising from the first of these sources could be corrected, in most cases, by measuring the distance from the center of percussion to the point of impact, and the second could be roughly corrected by weighing the fragments and assuming that they struck with the same velocity as the shot. It was thought best, however, to reject the results affected by these causes and to avoid the use of the ballistic pendulum as far as practicable by so arranging the striking velocity of the shot and thicknesses of the plates that the work of the shot would be nearly, if not quite, expended in penetration, and, when it failed to get through, measuring the work remaining to be done by forcing the same shot through the remaining distance in a testing machine, the strain being recorded for successive increments of penetration, as will be described in another place.

TESTING MACHINE.—The machine used in testing the tensile strength and other properties of metal was one of those designed by Major Wade, formerly of the Ordnance Corps U. S. A., and was built at the West Point foundry in 1852. A full description of this machine, with drawings, may be found in the "Reports on Metals for Cannon," published by the Ordnance Department in 1856.

This machine was arranged for short specimens only, and as the power was applied to the scale-beam which measures the strain, an arrangement which admitted of only a very slight stretch in the specimen, it was unsuited to the purpose of breaking specimens giving elongations of several inches. A change was therefore made in the lower fastening of the specimen, by which the power was applied at that point, through a screw and cog-wheels, and this arrangement was found to answer the purpose in the most satisfactory manner.

Another change was made in order to get a continuous increase in the weight upon the scale-beam instead of adding one weight at a time, as is generally done. This was accomplished by using a chain for a weight and reeling into the scale as fast as required to balance the strain upon the specimen. The principal advantage of this method was in working the indicator hereinafter described.

Another testing machine used for a portion of these experiments was that in the Ordnance Office at the Washington Navy Yard—a modification of the foregoing by General Rodman.

INDICATOR.—In connection with the testing machine it was found desirable to have an instrument which would give a continuous curve, representing the elongations and corresponding tensile strains for specimens of various kinds, in order to arrive at the exact dynamical value of the metal.

An instrument of this kind was devised for the purpose, and is shown on Plate II. It consists of a brass frame *A B*, supporting a vertical cylinder *C*, revolved by the endless screw *S*, this screw being turned by the tape *T*, which draws around the pulley *P*, as the weight *W* is moved along the scale-beam. When the chain was used as a weight, the cylinder revolved as the chain was paid into the scale.

This arrangement causes the cylinder to revolve as the weight or strain upon the specimen increases or diminishes, and if the marker M remains stationary it will describe a horizontal circle upon the paper with which the cylinder is covered. Starting from the zero point of the scale, the length of any arc of this circle will represent the strain upon the specimen at the instant the marker has arrived at the end of the arc.

If now the elongation of a given portion of the specimen carries the marker in a direction parallel to the axis of the cylinder, it is clear that the curve $N\,O$, described upon the paper, will accurately and continuously represent the relation between the elongation of the specimen and the corresponding strain upon it. In order to move the marker in this manner, it is connected with one end of the specimen by the clamp Q', which fits into a center-punch mark on the specimen, while the frame and cylinder are attached to the other end Q of the specimen in a similar manner.

The portion of the specimen between the two center-punch marks is evidently the only portion whose elongation will move the marker along the paper, and the space passed over by the marker divided by the original length of this portion will give the elongation per unit of length of the specimen, or the per cent. of elongation; and the area bounded by the curve $N\,O$, and the co-ordinates $N\,R$ and $R\,O$, measures the *work* of breaking the specimen.

Planimeter.—In measuring the areas bounded by irregular curves like those given by the instrument just described, or by forcing a shot or punch of any kind into metal, and measuring the resistance and corresponding penetration at different points, two methods were adopted; one was the usual method of ordinates, and the other by a small instrument known as *Amsler's Planimeter.*

A full description of this instrument and the principles upon which it operates will be found in Professor F. A. P. Barnard's Report on Apparatus of The Exact Sciences at the Paris Exposition of 1867. This instrument is very simple in its construction and operation, and gives sufficiently, though not rigidly, accurate results, with a great saving of time over ordinary methods.

Whirling Machine.—Although the gun-pendulum was supposed to give relative velocities sufficiently accurate when there were but little variations in the charge, it was thought best to use some other means to determine a few absolute velocities with which to compare its indications.

For this purpose two light wooden wheels, seven feet in diameter, were mounted on a horizontal axis twenty-five feet long and parallel with that of the gun. These wheels were provided with rims of paper projecting about four inches from their circumferences; the axis of the wheels being placed at such a level that the shot from the gun would pass through both these rims. By revolving this axis, the two wheels were made to revolve at the same rate, and this rate was ascertained by an attachment of clock-work.

When the wheels were revolving at a uniform velocity the gun was fired, the shot making holes through the paper rims and through stationary pieces of paper placed near each rim. The wheels being stopped and brought back so that the hole through one rim coincides with the hole in the stationary paper, the distance between the hole in the other rim and that in the corresponding stationary paper, is the chord of the arc passed through by the wheels, while the shot was passing through the distance between them.

The angular velocity of the wheels being known, the absolute velocity of the point through which the shot passed may be computed, and by a simple proportion the velocity of the shot becomes known. Thus, supposing the distance passed over by the point of the rim while the shot was passing through the distance between the rims, to have been one and a half feet, the velocity of the same point sixty feet, and the distance between the rims twenty-four feet, we have: $1\frac{1}{2} : 24 :: 60$: velocity of the shot, or 960 feet.

This apparatus, which was nearly the same as that used by Grobert many years ago, was adopted chiefly because of its being the only one available at the time; but for this purpose, and generally for determining the velocity of small projectiles, it would, with some slight modification, give results nearly, if not quite, as accurate as many of the more costly and complicated instruments, and it would be less liable to involve unknown and unlooked-for errors.

Sand Box.—In the experiments on penetration in sand, a sheet-iron cylinder, two feet in diameter and four feet long, was used, (Fig. 3, Plate I.) This cylinder was placed with its axis in the prolongation of the bore of the gun, and was filled through the upper side, which was left open for that purpose, the sand being allowed to take its own density. There was a hole three inches in diameter in one end of the cylinder, which was covered with rocket paper each time it was filled, to allow the shot to pass through into the sand without appreciable resistance.

It might appear that sand placed in a cylinder of this description would be confined to such an extent as to affect the amount of penetration; but, by comparing the diameter of the cylinder with the caliber of the gun, it will be seen that the depth of sand is much greater than the proportional depth likely to be met in practice with service guns. The diameter of the cylinder is twenty-four diameters of the shot, and this proportion applied to the 15-inch gun would give a cylinder thirty feet in diameter, which could have no appreciable effect upon a shot moving along its axis.

CUTTER.—In testing for hardness, one of the cutters from a Rodman pressure piston was used. (Figs. 4 & 5, Plate XXVII.) This cutter, it will be recollected, is of hardened steel, and of a pyramidal form, the angles at the edge being 57, and 163½ degrees.

This cutter was forced into specimens of the metal in the testing machine, and the work required to produce an indent of a given depth was taken as the measure of the hardness of the specimen.

Major Wade, formerly of the Ordnance Corps, applied a similar test to metals for cannon in 1850.

Another form of cutter was used, which consisted of a triangular pyramid, the faces being equal and the angles between edges being 47½ degrees. (Fig. 3, Plate XXVII.)

IMPACT OF PROJECTILES.

In order to arrive at a clear understanding of what takes place when the motion of a projectile is arrested by any resisting medium, it will be necessary to recall some of the elementary principles upon which these phenomena depend.

The manner in which a shot acquires its velocity is a good illustration of the manner in which its motion is destroyed. Although the effect of the explosion of gunpowder appears to be instantaneous, it is well known that it is a gradual, though very quick, process, and that the shot is acted upon by a continuous though variable pressure of the gas, from the instant the charge is ignited until the projectile leaves the bore of the gun. If the mean pressure of the gas be multiplied by the distance passed over by the shot while acquiring its velocity, the result will be the measure of the work done by the charge of powder; and it will also be equal to the work of stopping the same projectile, no matter how or by what means it may be brought to rest.

The same result may be arrived at, and generally is, by measuring the velocity imparted to the shot under the circumstances mentioned, and multiplying the square of this velocity by one-half the mass of the projectile; or, since the mass is equal to the weight divided by the force of gravity the expression for the work stored in the shot, and which must be expended in bringing the shot to rest $\frac{W.v^2}{2g}$, where

W = weight of the shot in pounds;

v = velocity of the shot in feet; and

g = the force of gravity in feet, or the velocity which a body will acquire by its own weight in one second of time.

This expression involves, indirectly, the same quantities as that first mentioned, namely, the mean pressure of the gas and the distance passed over by the shot; and assuming this measure for the work stored in the shot, it remains to consider how this work is expended.

The following are the different effects produced by the impact of a shot upon any solid body, some of these being so connected as to render their relative importance extremely doubtful.

1st. COMPRESSION.—The first effect of impact is to compress, or drive back, those portions of both shot and target first coming in contact, upon those immediately behind them, the amount of this compression of course depending upon the material and velocity of impact, as well as upon the form of the shot.

Even with soft wrought iron plates and flat-headed shot, it was found that the plug punched out was but slightly diminished in thickness, the compression in no case amounting to $\frac{1}{30}$ of the thickness of the plate, in the middle of the plug, and not exceeding $\frac{1}{8}$ at the edge.

2nd. ELONGATION.—The greater part of the work of the shot in penetrating wrought iron and similar materials is undoubtedly expended in overcoming the tenacity of the material or in elongating the fiber. This is evident when we consider that punching or shearing consists not so much in cutting the fiber as in bending it and afterward pulling it in two lengthwise.

By examining the fractured surface of the plugs punched out, as well as of the hole, it was found that the direction of the fiber had been bent nearly at right angles and almost parallel to the direction in which the shot moved. This was also shown by sections of the plugs, (Figs. 6, 7, and 8, Plate XXVII.)

3rd. SHEARING.—This, as just stated, consists chiefly in the two strains already mentioned.

4th. BENDING.—This also implies tension and compression, the back of the plate being elongated and the front compressed.

5th. PULVERIZING a portion of the material. This takes place only in case of hard materials, as stone or cast iron, and it then absorbs a very great amount of work. Like bending and shearing, it involves compression and elongation, the material being compressed until it yields laterally to a tensile strain.

6th. MOTION.—While the work is being expended a certain amount of time is allowed for the force of the shot to impart motion to the target, especially that portion immediately in front of the shot.

7th. FRICTION.—The friction is very great, especially in case of the more pointed forms of projectile, and probably varies inversely with the velocity of the shot.

8th. HEAT.—This is probably due to friction, both external and internal, that is of the shot and fragments against the plate and against each other, and of the particles of both shot and plate against each other during the distortion of the material from compression, bending, &c.

The suddenness with which this heat is generated is unequaled by any known source of heat, excepting, perhaps, electricity of high tension. It was found that fragments of wrought-iron plates and steel shot were frequently raised to a temperature of five or six hundred degrees Fahrenheit, as indicated by the color given to them, in the short space of time during which the shot was in contact with the plate. This time was not probably greater than $\frac{1}{1000}$ part of a second, and could this have been prolonged to $\frac{1}{64}$ of a second with a corresponding increase in temperature, the heat generated would have melted wrought iron; and about double that time, or say $\frac{1}{32}$ of a second, would have been sufficient to melt all known substances. It is well known that the heat developed in the interior of loaded shells, on striking a thick iron plate, is sometimes sufficient to ignite the powder, and this fact has been utilized by Mr. Whitworth in dispensing with fuzes for exploding armor-punching shells.

9th. SOUND WAVES, as well as ELECTRICITY, MAGNETISM, and LIGHT, are also generated, but are of no practical significance in this connection.

Were it possible to do so, the most accurate way to investigate these phenomena would be to make a series of experiments upon each by itself and ascertain exactly what portion of the work of the shot is absorbed by each, and also the conditions upon which their relative importance depend.

This course is, however, entirely out of the question, at least for the present.

The effect of a shot, on striking a mass or target of any form or material, may be divided into two general portions, one being entirely local, while the other is distributed over more or less surface, according to circumstances.

The former is the *penetration* and the latter may be called the *concussion* or jarring effect.

1—PENETRATION.

(a) General theory of penetration.

The circumstances attending the penetration of iron plates are analogous to those which obtain whenever the motion of a projectile is opposed by any resisting medium whatever, and the law of penetration for iron may therefore be treated as a particular case of a more general law, applicable to all materials. In fact, the resistances experienced by a projectile moving in air or water are but extreme cases of the same law, and we may write the following series in which the more common substances encountered by projectiles are arranged in the order of their resistances to penetration: *Air, water, sand, wood, lead, copper, wrought iron, soft steel, cast iron, chilled iron, hardened steel,* &c. All other substances may be arranged between these, or in continuation of the series.

Air opposes the motion of a projectile by its inertia, elastic force, and the pressure due to its weight. The shot compresses the air in its front and disperses it laterally, while the rear of the shot is relieved by its motion, of the normal pressure of the air. A small amount of resistance is also met with in the shape of friction.

In the case of *water* these resistances are increased by the greater density and weight of this substance, and there is also a slight additional resistance due to the viscosity or cohesion among the particles.

Sand being a solid, or at least made up of solid elements, presents the additional resistance of "crushing strength." It cannot be penetrated at a high velocity without crushing some of the grains, and the higher the velocity the greater the amount of work expended in this manner. This resistance to crushing implies a continuation of the elastic force beyond the elastic limits, and involves, indirectly, tensile strength; since a solid, in being crushed, must enlarge laterally and finally yield to a strain of tension.

In penetrating *wood, lead,* or any of the other materials, "tensile strength" forms the chief element of the resistance, while inertia and friction become of minor importance.

The office of elasticity in all these cases is to transmit the effect of the shot from those particles first acted upon to those more remote, and thus calling into play their inertia or tensile strength, as the case may be; and, were it not for this property the statical resistance of a plate of any material to perforation would be entirely independent of the thickness of the plate. In other words, a thick plate would offer no greater resistance than a thin one, since each layer or unit of thickness would be perforated without receiving any assistance from its neighbors. The *work* of penetration would then vary directly with the distance penetrated, or the thickness of the plate.

It should be borne in mind, however, that elasticity has its maximum point of usefulness in resisting penetration, and beyond this it becomes a great disadvantage. While increasing the number of fibers or elementary portions of the material broken at once, thereby increasing the statical resistance, it diminishes the time during which this resistance opposes the motion of the shot in like ratio, and the amount of motion destroyed or generated increases with the time as well as with the force or resistance. For this reason hardened steel and chilled iron are less efficient in stopping projectiles than soft iron, although they offer a much greater statical resistance to penetration.

There are many reasons for believing that a general formula for the penetration of shot in all materials may be deduced, when experiments have been sufficiently extended, in which the constants will simply require changing to suit any particular case under consideration. As the number of materials is much greater than the number of physical properties of materials necessary to be taken into account, it would probably simplify the matter to make the constants depend upon the physical properties without reference to the materials themselves. That is, instead of deducing a set of constants for *iron*, another for *wood*, and so on, let the constants depend upon the density, tensile strength, elasticity, &c.

Several points tending to establish this view have been suggested during the course of these experiments; but they have not, as yet, taken a form sufficiently definite to warrant further notice in this place.

(b) *Formula for perforation of iron plates.*

One of the first questions to present itself in connection with armor-plating is the relation between the thickness of the plate and the diameter, weight, and velocity of the projectile required to perforate it; or, having given the diameter, weight, and velocity of a projectile, required the thickness of a single wrought-iron plate which it will just perforate.

Several formulæ have been proposed for this purpose, but the great difficulty has been the want of experimental results, sufficiently accurate and comprehensive to verify the principles upon which they were based, and to give the correct values for the constants or coefficients which enter them.

Perhaps the best mode of arriving at a proper understanding of the question will be by a discussion of one of these formulæ.

In his "Report on various experiments carried out under the direction of the ordnance select committee, relative to the penetration of iron armor plates by steel shot," Captain Noble, R. A., gives the following formula for the penetration of wrought-iron plates by steel shot, the impact being direct.

$$\frac{W \cdot v^2}{2g} = 2 \cdot \pi R k b^2, \text{ where}$$

W = weight of shot in pounds.

v = velocity on impact, in feet.

g = the force of gravity.

$2R$ = diameter of shot in feet.

b = thickness of unbacked plate, in feet.

k = a coefficient, depending on the nature of the wrought iron in the plate and the nature and form of head of the shot.

It is proposed to examine the principles upon which this formula is based. These principles are stated by Captain Noble, as follows:

1st. "An unbacked wrought-iron plate will be perforated with equal facility by solid steel shot, of similar form of head, and having the same diameter, provided they have the same vis viva on impact; and it is immaterial whether this vis viva be the result of a heavy shot and low velocity or a light shot and high velocity, within the usual limits of length, &c., which occur in practice."

The clause limiting this rule to service projectiles is apparently a saving clause; but the reason for this limitation, given in a note at the bottom of the page, that "if the elongated shot be of excessive length there will be a waste of work in altering the form of the shot itself," is not the *only* reason why the rule is not strictly true.

Another reason is that the work expended in bending or buckling the plate is the greater as the velocity of the shot is less; provided, of course, that the whole amount of work expended is constant.

This is owing to the fact that with the lower velocity the time during which the resistance is acting is greater, and as the resistance itself is also rather greater in the same case, the quantity of motion generated in the plate will necessarily be greater; which amounts to saying that the plate will be either bent more or moved bodily to the rear.

For example, a spherical shot weighing 100 pounds, striking with a velocity of 1,000 feet per second, will do an amount of work represented by $\frac{100\times 1{,}000^2}{2g}$; while a cylindro-spherical shot of the same diameter, and say four times the weight, would require only 500 feet velocity to have the same work, since $\frac{100\times 1{,}000^2}{2g}=\frac{400\times 500^2}{2g}$.

Now the resistance met with in penetrating any given plate will be somewhat less for the spherical shot, while the time during which it is acting will be only one-half what it is for the elongated shot, and the plate will be therefore bent more than twice as much in the latter as in the former case

It is found that in practice we may meet with cases where one-half of the entire work of the shot is expended in bending the plate, and it follows from what has preceded, that one-half of this amount, or one-fourth of the whole work, might be in error by the application of the rule in question.

It may appear that this supposes a greater variation in velocity than the rule was intended to cover, but it will be noticed that the following rule, taken in connection with the foregoing, gives a very wide range in velocities.

For example, the velocity required to send a spherical shot through an eight-inch plate may be compared with the velocity which would send a cylindro-spherical shot of three times the weight through a two-inch plate, in which case there must of course be a great difference in velocities. In fact, in the tables given by Captain Noble, the velocities vary from 710 to 1,925 feet per second.

In order to get a true expression for the work of penetration, the whole work expended by the shot must, therefore, be diminished by a quantity increasing with the whole work and diminishing with the velocity of impact; or, $\frac{A.W.v^2}{2g.v} = \frac{A.W.v}{2g}$ in which "A" is a quantity of the same kind as v and depending upon the size and form of shot and upon the dimensions of the plate, distance between supports, and several other conditions not necessary to enumerate; W. v. and g—same as before. Indicating the subtraction of the above quantity from the expression for the whole work expended, and we have the following equation $\frac{W.v^2}{2g} - \frac{A.W.v}{2g} = X$........................(1)

That is, the whole work — the smashing effect = the work of penetration.

If the elements upon which the value of A depends be so taken that A is very small in comparison with v, the second term of the above equation will disappear, or the whole work will be expended in punching. An example of this would be a musket ball fired through a window pane. If on the other hand A is equal to v the whole work is expended in smashing or bending the plate and upsetting the shot. It should have been stated that the value of the second term may include the work done upon the shot as well as upon the plate.

The value of A has been determined for a few particular cases during these experiments, (rounds No. 325 and 326, Plate XVIII,) and it is believed that it may in practice be found under some circumstances to exceed one-half of v or $\frac{v}{2}$, which in equation (1) gives $X = \frac{W v^2}{4g}$; or one-half of the whole work is expended in penetration and the other half in smashing, bending, &c.

From the foregoing it appears that in order to attain a maximum effect in either punching or smashing, the shot should be adapted to one purpose only.

2nd. "An unbacked iron plate will be penetrated by solid steel shot, of the same form of head but different diameters, provided their striking vis viva varies as the diameter, nearly, that is, as the circumference of the shot."

This rule is not strictly true, though as yet we have not sufficient data for correcting it. There is however good reason to believe that the work of penetration varies partly with the diameter and partly with the square of the diameter of the shot; the latter term being much smaller than the former.

To illustrate, suppose a series of very thin, hollow cylinders of different diameters but of equal thickness to be fired or punched through an iron plate. The resistances will evidently be proportional to their diameters. Now let these cylinders be plugged up or made solid, and an additional resistance will be met with in each case proportional to the area of the plug or the square of the diameter, since the plug will have to compress the metal in the middle while the edge is cutting its way through. Plate IV, Figs. 3 and 4.

3rd "That the resistance of unbacked wrought-iron plates to absolute penetration by solid steel shot of similar form and equal diameter, varies as the square of their thickness nearly." The note at the bottom of the page states as a condition that the plates must be of good iron.

The question arises, does the "resistance to penetration," or, more properly, the *work of perforation*, vary with the square of the thickness; and if so, why?

From page 7 of Captain Noble's report, it appears that this law was established by assuming it to be true, and computing from the experiments on a 5½-inch plate the amount of work necessary to perforate a 4½-inch plate, and then firing a single shot at the 4½-inch plate to verify the result.

Further, in order to determine the value of k, the constant in his formulæ, he makes the following transpositions. (Page 9.)

$$4.\ \pi.\ R_1\ g.\ b^2\ k. - W_1\ r_1^2 = O.$$
$$4.\ \pi.\ R_2\ g.\ b^2\ k. - W_2\ r_2^2 = O.$$
$$4.\ \pi.\ R_3\ g.\ b^2\ k - W_3\ r_3^2 = O.$$
&c. &c. &c.

From which he says, "Substituting the experimental values of the different quantities and eliminating k, we find that for hemispherical-headed shot $k = 5357200$."

The variable quantities in these equations are R. b. W. and v; π being the usual representative of the ratio of diameter to circumference of the circle, and g representing the force of gravity in dynamical terms.

It will be noticed that the "*Subs.*" 1, 2, and 3 are omitted from b^2 in these equations, from which it would appear that b was not varied in deducing the value of k; in other words, that this value was obtained from experiments against plates of one thickness only. The correct way would have been to have varied b as well as R, W, and v, as much as possible, and if the equation had been a true one the values of k would have been *nearly* the same for each set of values for the other quantities, (it would have been exactly the same but for unavoidable errors and differences in making the experiments,) and from the slightly discordant values the most probable mean value could have been obtained.

It is found, however, by selecting all the applicable data from Captain Noble's report, and from other experiments, that each value of b, with the corresponding values of the other quantities, gives a different value for k, and these discrepancies are so great as to indicate that b^2 is not, excepting perhaps within narrow limits, the proper function to express the law of variation of the thickness of the plate for the indicated variations of the other quantities in the equation.

Other reasons for this conclusion will appear in the deduction of a new equation, and it is due to Captain Noble that it should be borne in mind that he does not claim perfect accuracy for his formula, but that it is a "near approximation."

In fact, the case is one which does not admit of absolute accuracy, involving as it does many sources of error and uncertainty which it is impossible to eliminate without an almost interminable series of experiments.

The laws of motion of a projectile in air, or even of a vessel in water, have never been reduced to exact mathematical language. In fact, since these experiments were commenced, it has been announced that the resistance of the air to a projectile varies more nearly with the cube, than with the square of the velocity as formerly supposed.

If the application of mathematics to the plainer questions of physical science has presented insurmountable difficulties, we may well despair of an exact solution to a question which presents many such difficulties combined.

It is thought, however, that a *nearer* approximation may be obtained in the following manner:

(c) *Deduction of New Formula.*

Assuming that the work of penetration has been separated, as far as practicable, from the work of bending the plate, upsetting the shot, &c., in accordance with the foregoing discussion, and that, in the absence of reliable data to the contrary, the resistance to punching, other circumstances being equal, increases directly with the diameter of the punch, we will proceed to deduce the relation between the thickness of the plate and the work of perforation.

The work of penetrating a plate may be represented graphically by the diagram, Fig. I, Plate XXI. Taking the front line of the plate and the axis of the shot for co-ordinate axes, and erecting at the point of the shot in its successive positions, ordinates representing the resistances offered by the plate at each point, a curve (a, b, c, d) is obtained which bounds an area representing the whole work of perforation.

Thus, when the point of the shot arrives at a, or just touches the plate, the resistance is evidently zero, when it reaches z the resistance is represented by the ordinate (z, b,) and so on for each successive point reached until finally at some point d the resistance ceases entirely and the perforation is complete.

The area (a, b, c, d, z) represents the work of perforation, and if we could deduce a value for this area, in terms of the thickness of the plate and diameter of the shot, the problem would be solved by simply placing this value equal to the expression for the work of the shot; thus $\frac{W. v^2}{2 g} = f(d, t.)$ in which d represents the diameter of the shot and t the thickness of the plate. But such a solution, if possible at all, would probably involve complicated mathematical expressions which would render it unsuitable for a practical formula.

In order to get a fair approximate solution we will suppose the plate made up of parallel laminæ of indefinitely small but uniform thickness and united to form a solid mass.

If, now, we consider the work of a unit, say one inch, of the shot's circumference, we are independent of the diameter of the shot, subject, of course, to the same liability to error that was mentioned in the discussion of Captain

Noble's second law, (Page 23.) and this quantity of work, which we will call Z, is equal to the distance passed over by the shot during the penetration, multiplied by some mean resistance.

The distance passed over must vary nearly with the thickness of the plate, for a given form of projectile, and the mean resistance must also be a function of that thickness, or $Z = t \times f(t)$........................(2) hence it only remains to find the form of this function expressing the mean resistance in terms of the thickness of the plate.

All the laminæ of which we have supposed the plate to consist cannot contribute equally in making up the mean resistance; for we know that under certain circumstances, as, for example, a very thick plate or a high velocity of shot, the rear laminæ will not be disturbed until the shot has penetrated for some distance and completely severed the laminæ first acted upon. This is owing to the fact that it requires *time* for the resistance or molecular forces to be transmitted through the metal.

If this molecular disturbance travels in wrought iron at a rate of 18,000 feet per second, and the shot strikes with a velocity of 1,200 feet, it is plain that while the resistance is traveling fifteen inches the shot will have penetrated nearly one inch. (It would be just one inch but for the fact that the shot is constantly losing velocity during penetration.) The rear laminæ will, therefore, offer no resistance until the shot has penetrated nearly one inch.

Even when the shot moves at a very slow rate, the force is not transmitted through, so as to allow the rear laminæ to exert their full strength in resisting penetration. This was shown by the results of punching in the testing machine, where it was found that the statical resistance increases less rapidly than the thickness of the plate.

The rear laminæ, therefore, do not assist as much in making up the mean resistance as those at the front, while the intermediate ones take an intermediate part; and there must be some law of continuity expressing the relation between these circumstances.

What is the most probable form of this law? Taking the usual rectangular co-ordinates and letting x represent the distance of any lamina from the front of the plate, and y the assistance contributed by this lamina in making up the mean resistance, we may suppose—

1st. $y = a$; x being indeterminate: which gives a right line parallel to the axis of X. (Fig. 2, Plate XXI.)

In this case each lamina affords the same assistance as the first one, which is the supposition upon which Captain Noble's formula is based, and which has been shown to be erroneous.

2nd. $y = a - b\,x$, which is also the equation of a right line, but making an angle with the axis of X. (Fig. 3, Plate XXI.)

Here we have each lamina offering an assistance equal to the one immediately preceding, minus a constant quantity. This is an improvement on the first supposition, but it is evident that the difference between consecutive laminæ should diminish as the laminæ are farther from the front of the plate, and this is expressed by the following equation.

3rd. $y = \frac{a}{b+x}$, which is the equation of an hyperbola referred to one of its asymptotes, and a line parallel to the other. (Fig. 4, Plate XXI.)

The assistance contributed by different laminæ are inversely proportional to their distances from a fixed point. As this form of the equation of continuity is the simplest one which will answer the purpose, and there are no data to show that any other form is called for by the circumstances of the case or will give more accurate results, it is adopted as the one best suited to the present purpose.

It will be observed that by giving proper values to the constants a and b, the direction and position of the curve with reference to the laminæ may be changed at pleasure. The values of these constants will be found and discussed after the formula is completed.

Resuming the equation $y = \frac{a}{b+x}$ and calling the thickness of each lamina dx, we have for the whole mean resistance $\int_0^t y.dx$, or substituting for y its value in the equation just given and writing $f\,(t)$ for mean resistance, we have $f\,(t) = \int_0^t \frac{a\,dx}{b+x} = a.\log\left(\frac{t}{b}+1\right)$ and this value for $f\,(t)$ in equation 2 gives $Z = a\,t.\log\left(\frac{t}{b}+1\right)$

The logarithm indicated in this equation belongs to the Napierian system, but by multiplying by (M) the modulus of the common system, we may use the latter and $Z = a.M.t.\log\left(\frac{t}{b}+1\right)$

The product of the two constants a. and M. may be represented by a new constant (a') and $\left(\frac{1}{b}\right)$ in the parenthesis may be replaced by $(b'.)$ hence $Z = a'.t.\log(b'\,t + 1;)$ and since this is the final equation or formula we may omit the primes and write $Z = a.\,t.\log(b.\,t + 1,)$ ....(3) in which it will be remembered.

Z = the quantity of work per inch of shot's circumference required to perforate the plate.

t = thickness of plate in inches.

a. and b = constants to be determined from the results of experiments.

In order to determine the values of these constants the following experimental results have been selected, and it is believed that they embrace all the results given in Captain Noble's report, which are applicable to the subject.

Where shot have failed to get through or where they have gone through with considerable but unknown velocities, the data can be of no use excepting to serve as limits within which the required values will be found.

The results used in deducing the values of a. and b. are marked with a star in the table.

TABLE I.

t. or Thickness of plate.	Z. or Work per inch of shot's circumference.	Remarks.
8 inches.	80.05 foot-tons.	Mean of *two* rounds: "Shot appears to be just through plate; shot badly broken up."
5.5 inches.	41.93 foot-tons.	Mean of *six* rounds: All went through with some little remaining velocity.
Do.	40.71 foot-tons. *	Mean of *three* rounds: Appear to have been just sufficient to perforate the plate.
4.5 inches.	27.98 foot-tons. *	Mean of *seven* rounds: Same.
3. inches.	14.2 foot-tons.	Mean of *three* rounds: Not through.
2.5 inches.	11.85 foot-tons.	Mean of *two* rounds: "Through and three feet six inches into earth."

With the exception of the first two rounds, the shot were either spherical or cylindro-spherical, and it will be seen that with the exception of three rounds fired at the 5.5-inch plate, and seven at the 4.5-inch plate, there are no definite data from which to deduce the values of a and b. We may infer however from the first two rounds, which were fired at the 8-inch plate on a Warrior backing, that about eighty foot-tons per inch of circumference will send a shot through an 8-inch plate, although it is by no means certain. From the three rounds against the 3-inch plate, we find that 11.2 foot-tons will not send a shot through that plate; and from the two at the 2.5-inch plate it is equally apparent that 11.8 foot-tons are more than are required to perforate a 2.5-inch plate.

In addition to the foregoing, the small experiments give for the half-inch plate, $Z=0.50$ foot-tons; for the three-quarter-inch, $Z=0.95$ foot-tons, and for 1-inch, $Z=1.61$ foot-tons.

Resuming equation (3) and solving with respect to a, we have $a=\frac{Z}{t\log(bt+1)}$, and substituting values from the table for Z and t, we may write $a=\frac{Z}{t\log(bt+1)}=\frac{Z'}{t'\log(bt'+1)}$; from which $\frac{Z\,t'}{Z'\,t}=\frac{\log(bt+1)}{\log(bt'+1)}$, which is independent of a, and from which the value of b may be obtained, and this substituted in the original equation gives a value for a. This operation repeated as many times as there are sets of values for Z and t, gives corresponding values for a and b, from which their most probable mean values may be obtained. In this manner it has been found that $a=39$, and $b=0.1$, nearly, which in equation (3) gives $Z=39t.\log(0.1t+1)$ .... (4)

Although this equation gives the value of Z directly for any assumed value for t, it is not so convenient when Z is given and t is required. In order to simplify this operation, and afford the means of comparing the two formulas, the curves (Plate XXIII) have been constructed, one from Captain Noble's formula and the other from the equation just given.

To ascertain the thickness of plate necessary to resist a shot of given weight, diameter, and velocity, by means of these curves, the expression for work per inch of shot's circumference may be placed in the following form, by simply substituting numerical values for the constants π and g, and reducing.

$$Z=\frac{W.v^2}{152{,}617d}\ \text{.......................... (5.)}$$

In which $W.$ and $v.$ represent the weight and velocity of the shot, as before, and d represents the diameter of the shot *in inches*, allowance being made in this reduction for the change of unit from feet to inches, from radius to diameter, and from pounds to tons.

These terms seem more convenient, as the diameter of the shot is generally given in inches; and to obtain the radius in feet requires computation. Substituting any given values of W., v., and d., in equation (5) we have the corresponding value of Z. Lay off an abscissa of the curve to represent this value, and the corresponding ordinate will be the thickness of the plate which would just be perforated.

A few examples are given in a table on the plate, which are believed to be the extreme limits of power thus far derived from the guns mentioned.

2. Concussion.

It has already been mentioned that the impact of a shot, in addition to indenting or penetrating a target, produces more or less bending, tearing, and other damage at a distance from the point of impact. These effects, which may be classed under the term "concussion," depend upon so many conditions and involve so many unknown and incommensurable quantities as to be almost exempt from an experimental or even a theoretical investigation; but a brief allusion to some of the more important points involved may aid in a solution of the matter.

But few experiments have been made in this direction, either in this series or in any of the larger experiments upon armor-plating, and the following conclusions are therefore presented as deductions from the fundamental principles of mechanics rather than from experimental results, though many of the points were suggested incidentally by these experiments:

1st. The effect of concussion is transmitted from the point of impact in all directions, in the same manner as sound waves, and increases with the elasticity of the material. Of course whatever tends to diminish the elasticity of the structure, as dividing it into many pieces, or using soft ductile material to receive the shot, will diminish the effect of concussion.

2nd. This effect is expended in two ways: first, in giving motion to the structure, or in developing inertia; and second, in overcoming the tenacity of the material, either in bending or in tearing those portions first acted upon from those more remote—that is, in breaking bolts and other fastenings.

3rd. Both of these components increase with the whole amount of work expended by the shot, other conditions being equal.

4th. The former being motion converted into motion, is nearly independent of the amount of penetration. It would be absolutely independent but for the fact that where the penetration is very slight the shot or pieces of it may be thrown to the rear by the elasticity of the metal, and this effect reacting upon the target would be in addition to that due to the stopping of the shot. Taking an extreme case, suppose the plate and shot to be perfectly elastic, and to resist all penetration: the shot would be thrown to the rear with nearly the velocity with which it struck, and the velocity imparted to the plate would be double what it would have been had the plate and shot been perfectly *inelastic*.

5th. The latter component will evidently increase as the amount of penetration diminishes, since the less the penetration the greater must be the force exerted by the structure to absorb a given amount of work from the shot; but the amount of penetration for the same form of shot, and with other conditions equal, diminishes nearly as the diameter of the shot increases; and since the work stored in a shot varies directly with its weight, or the cube of the diameter, we may conclude that *that portion of the effect of concussion expended in overcoming the cohesion of the material varies directly with the fourth power of the diameter of the shot.* On this supposition this effect for the 10, 15, and 20-inch spherical shot would be as 1, 5, and 16, respectively, whereas the relative penetrations of these shot would be only about as 1, 1½, and 2.

6th. The same effect may also be shown to vary directly with the velocity of impact. For a given amount of work expended by the shot it is evident that the lower the velocity, or the longer the time allowed for the force or resistance of the target to work, and the concussion to be transmitted to distant points, the greater will be the effect in bending the target, breaking bolts, and otherwise shattering the structure; but the whole work varies with the square of the velocity, and this divided by the velocity leaves the first power of the velocity, as before stated.

The mathematical expression for this portion of the effect of concussion would be $X = C. D^2. E. V$ .... (6)
in which

X = the effect in question;

C = a constant or coefficient;

D = the diameter of the shot;

E = the mean coefficient of elasticity of shot and target; and

V = the velocity of impact.

The form of shot is supposed to be the same in all cases. The effect of changing the form would depend upon the change in penetration; those forms giving the greatest penetration giving the least effect of concussion.

Some experiments were made to determine the amount of bending which might occur in certain cases during the penetration.

For this purpose strips of wrought iron three inches wide, twelve inches long, and from one-half inch to one inch thick, were supported at points eleven inches apart and fired at with different forms of shot.

(See rounds Nos. 47, 325, and 326, Plate XVIII.)

The results show:

1st. That a one-half-inch plate of the width stated will be no nearer perforated, if allowed to bend, than a three-quarter-inch-plate of the same iron if held firmly or made of sufficient width to resist much bending. In other words, that about one-half the work of the shot was expended in bending the plate.

2nd. That the amount of bending increases directly with the velocity until the work of the shot becomes sufficient to perforate the plate, after which it diminishes as the velocity increases.

3rd. That the bending of the plate due to cylindrical shot is much less than when cylindro-spherical, or ogival shot are used, the velocities being the same, and the work stored in the shot being sufficient in either case to perforate the plate.

Effect of Concussion or Vibration on the Structure of Metal.

It is a very generally accepted theory that iron or steel, however fibrous or lamellar, may be instantly changed to a crystalline structure by a sudden impact, or gradually changed by often repeated strains or vibrations; and this theory has been brought forward on numerous occasions to account for the breaking of machinery, car axles, railway bars, and other masses of iron, as well as to throw distrust upon the durability of steel rails, suspension bridges, and other structures supposed to be liable to this source of danger.

There can be no doubt of the fact that iron suddenly broken, or broken after long-continued vibration, does often present a crystalline fracture as far as can be judged from appearances. The question then is, do the crystals actually exist, and if so, are they the result of impact or vibration after the metal has taken its solid form? It is believed that crystallization can only take place when the free particles of a *fluid* are allowed to take their choice of positions in the process of forming a solid body. In good wrought iron these conditions are as far from existing as can well be imagined.

The crystals of the iron formed after the puddling process, are drawn out into fibers or flattened into laminæ and cemented together by slag or cinder during the process of shingling, fagoting, and rolling: the different particles which constitute the same crystal, being thus mechanically distributed along the bar for distances which may in some cases amount to several inches. Now in order that the proper elements of such a mass may be brought together to form a new crystal, whether they are the identical ones which formed the original crystals or not, it is evident that some of them must travel through an appreciable distance of solid metal, this distance increasing with the size of the crystals formed and the amount of drawing out which the bar has undergone. This we know to be impossible, since the most powerful microscopes have failed to reveal the slightest motion among the particles of a solid body, although it is generally admitted that the ultimate atoms of which all bodies are composed do have certain motions among their immediate neighbors.

To show that good fibrous wrought iron is not homogeneous it may be mentioned that a bar thrust into the intense flame of a Siemens' furnace, instead of being melted down at once like a piece of cast iron or lead, is melted in seams, which were evidently the original welds formed in piling the mass from which the bar was rolled. The appearance of a bar thus melted is therefore something like a splint broom, the splints being the separate bars of which the whole bar was made.

This experiment also throws some light upon the subject of welding, and I think the conclusion may be safely drawn that the borax and silica used in that process and which are supposed to simply protect the surface of the iron from oxidation and thus give clean surfaces for welding, perform the far more important office of fluxes to render the surface of the metal more fusible than the interior; so that the exterior of the bars to be welded are actually melted and run together while the interior is still in a solid state. This view is still further corroborated by the fact that cast iron skillfully treated may be welded in a similar manner, though of course it must not be hammered after the parts are united.

The theory of the formation of crystals under the conditions mentioned may be accounted for in the following manner:

1st. The crystals may actually exist before the fracture takes place, or, in other words, they may be *revealed* instead of being *formed* by the impact. This should not of course be the case with good fibrous wrought iron, but in large forgings it often occurs that the crystalline form is not entirely destroyed, and the same state of things may result from forging small bars when not at a proper and uniform heat.

2nd. The *appearance* of a crystalline structure may result from the suddenness of the fracture, in which case inertia plays an important part in determining the surface of fracture. When a beam is broken the fibers are broken successively, beginning with those on the side of greatest tension. When one fiber is parted the strain which it sustained is thrown upon its next neighbor, which in turn is broken, and the several fractures of the fibers form the surface of fracture of the beam. If this operation is performed by a slow and steady application of force, it is evident that each fiber will have a tendency to break at its weakest point, and as these weak points would not be likely to fall in the same plane or in fact in any regular or even surface, the result will be a jagged or fibrous-looking fracture. An illustration of this is shown at A. B., Fig. 2, Plate XXIV. On the other hand let the strain be suddenly applied, and the edge of fracture as it passes from fiber to fiber will have no time to seek out, as it were, the weakest point of each fiber, but it will take a shorter cut and the result may be a surface so even as to be readily mistaken for a crystalline fracture. (C. D., Fig. 2, Plate XXIV.) A good, though somewhat exaggerated, illustration of the different effect of slow and quick applications of force in producing fractures is the common molasses candy or "taffy." By a steady pull it may be drawn out into a single fiber as fine as a thread of silk, but a slight rap with the back of a knife will break a mass of it with a fracture almost as smooth as glass.

3rd. A shiny crystalline appearance may occur from the gradual wearing of the parts in case of a partial fracture which is subsequently parted, or where during the operation of breaking the parts are forcibly rubbed together. An example of the first would be a car axle which had been run for some time after being partially broken; and of the second, certain parts of a shot which are forcibly rubbed together after the fracture and before the shot has expended its force.

Crystalline structure, though not desirable in case of wrought iron, is not an infallible sign of weakness. Some metals, as Bessemer steel cut from the ingot without reheating, and containing but little more carbon than wrought iron, exhibited a coarse crystalline fracture and yet gave a greater tensile strength than the most fibrous iron. The elongation was, however, considerably less than that of the iron.

While it is highly improbable that the weakness of structures sometimes exhibited on sudden impact, and the gradual deterioration said to take place in other cases from jars and vibrations, can be due to crystallization as before stated, the facts themselves still remain; though it is to be hoped that the disconnection of the mysterious phenomenon of crystallization from them may throw some light upon their causes and remedies.

Continued vibration, whether from impact or other causes, undoubtedly injures the tenacity of metals; but in order to produce an appreciable effect in a reasonable length of time, the extent of vibration or bending must be such as to stretch, at least the extreme fibers, beyond their elastic limits, at each vibration.

The manner of weakening a beam by repeated bendings, may be illustrated by reference to Fig. 3, Plate XXIV.

Let the beam *A B* be held rigidly from *A* to *C*, while the end *B* is made to vibrate from *B′* to *B″*. The greatest bending will take place at the cross section *C D*. When the end of the beam is at *B′* a fiber at *D* will be elongated, and one at *C* will be compressed.

If we suppose the extent of neither of these disturbances to exceed what the fiber will endure without taking a permanent set, no harm will be done the beam. But if, on the other hand, a permanent elongation of a fiber at D takes place it is evident that this fiber must be subject to an equal amount of compression when the end of the beam comes back to B; and whatever may be the arrangement of the elementary portions of the fiber, it is next to impossible that the compression should bring these elements back to the exact position they occupied before the elongation took place, since the portion of the fiber most extended would not necessarily be the part most susceptible to compression.

As the bending continues and the end arrives at B'' the foregoing operation is repeated in the inverse order, but at least a portion of its effect will be added to that already produced, and this effect will thus continue to be augmented by the successive vibrations until the tenacity of the fiber is entirely destroyed; meanwhile, the strain which this fiber is no longer able to bear is transferred to those next in order, which added to the strain they have already, as integral parts of the whole beam, causes them to undergo the same destructive process, but in shorter times, in consequence of the increased strain acting upon them. The same process, acting upon the other fibers successively, will destroy them in constantly decreasing time, and finally complete the rupture of the beam.

Thus the hairspring of a watch or the circuit-breaker of an induction coil often endure millions of vibrations without the slightest indication of weakness, while the same pieces of metal, if bent so as to take a *set*, indicating that the elastic limits of some of the fibers have been passed, would be broken by comparatively few vibrations.

The same is true in regard to impact. Even cast iron will endure an indefinite number of light blows of a hammer, but as the force of the blow is increased, the number of blows resisted diminishes in a very high ratio.

In fact, it is hard to conceive of any material being employed in such a manner as to exempt it entirely from vibration—sound waves, if nothing more; and it is evident that while there are no absolute and well-defined elastic limits, there are practical limits, which may be approached with perfect safety. The fact that there are no well-defined limits, instead of throwing distrust upon all applications of metal where vibrations are looked for, is an argument against the necessity for such limits. I believe, therefore, that any structure whatever will endure indefinitely any amount of vibration, whether produced from concussion or repeated strains, provided a proper margin of safety is allowed.

The competition among contractors and builders, and their desire to underbid each other in making proposals for work, undoubtedly leads to a disregard of this provision, and unless restrained by legislation, will eventually manifest itself by the rapid increase in the number of accidents from falling buildings, bridges, and other structures.

In fact, such accidents are not rare at the present time, and our cities and thoroughfares are well supplied with structures ready to avail themselves of the slightest excuse for manifesting their weakness.

OBLIQUE IMPACT.

The results of some experiments on this subject are shown on Plates XIX and XX, from which it will be seen that the angle of incidence was increased from 45° to 87°, or the angle between the axis of the shot and the surface of the plate was reduced from 45° to 3°.

Some of the plates were backed with hickory plank 1¼ inches thick while others were simply supported at the edges, as in the experiments in direct firing.

Perhaps the most important fact developed by these experiments was that flat-headed shot will "bite into" a plate when moving almost parallel with its surface. Rounds Nos. 473 and 474, Plate XX, show that when the angle between the axis of the shot and the surface of the plate was reduced to only 3°, the edge of the shot cut into the plate.

Now, if similar results can be attained with service guns, suppose a monitor to have taken a position at a distance of 2,000 feet from a battery 100 feet high. A line drawn at a depression of about 3° from this battery will just strike the monitor, and if the deck of the monitor be 250 feet long by 50 feet wide, it will present the appearance, at the battery, of a vertical target 12.5 feet high by 50 feet wide when the monitor is head-on, and 2.5 feet high and 250 feet wide when she is broadside to the battery. In the first position, or head-on, she could be struck without difficulty by well-served rifle guns, and, since the shot moves in a curved line, it would strike at an angle slightly greater than 3°, which would insure a hole in the deck unless heavily plated. In the second position, or broadside, the chances of hitting would be diminished, but the possibility of perforating the deck would still remain.

If the vessel should come within 1,000 feet of the same battery the deck would present about twice the area, or a target 25 feet high by 50 feet broad, which could easily be hit in the majority of cases; and since the shot would strike at an angle of about 6°, the perforation of the deck would be almost certain.

Experiments in this direction were suggested by General Humphreys.

Let it be required to cover by armor-plating a perpendicular surface, of which *A B*, Fig. 6, Plate XXI, is a vertical section, in the most advantageous manner, with respect to the slope of the plate. If, now, *a A* represents the thickness of plating necessary to stop all projectiles when the impact is direct, the rectangle *a B* will represent the section of a vertical plate which will properly cover the given surface. Since this plate is proof against direct impact it will certainly stop all projectiles striking it obliquely The parallelograms *a B'* and *a B''* having equal bases and altitudes, will have the same area as *a B*, which amounts to saying that plates occupying the positions *A B'* or *A B''* and of the thickness represented, would contain the same quantity of metal, and, so far as the present discussion is concerned, would be equally expensive.

It is also evident that a shot moving in a horizontal line (*d f*) would pass through the same thickness of metal in perforating either of the three plates, and the fractured area being also the same, provided of course that the shot continues in a horizontal line, it is contended by some that no advantage is gained by giving the plate an inclination to the horizon, while the vertical plating is simpler, easier of construction, and gives more convenient form to the interior of the work or space covered by the plating. This, however, cannot be correct so far as penetration is concerned, since whatever may be the form of the shot, it will be deflected more or less in penetrating the plate.

If the plate and shot were both perfectly elastic, and both resisted the impact, the shot would rebound in the direction of the line *C g;* the line *b C* being normal to the plate, and the angle *b C g* being equal to *b C d*. Since neither the plate nor shot *are* perfectly elastic, the shot will, if it fails to perforate the plate, rebound in some direction, *C h*, between the lines *C g* and the surface of the plate: and if it *does* perforate, the same force which deflected it in the former cases is still acting, only with a less degree of intensity, and the shot will therefore take some direction, *C C*, in which it must pass through a greater thickness of metal than it would have done in perforating the vertical plate.

The actual path of the shot in passing through the plate is a reverse curve, as shown by the dotted lines *i k* and *J K'*, the direction on leaving the plate being downward, and the amount of this deflection in both directions being dependent upon the velocity of the shot, thickness and quality of the plate, angle of incidence, and upon the particular nature of the fracture produced as the shot progresses in its work. This last depends upon the direction in which the fiber of the iron runs with respect to the plane of incidence, the deflection being greater when the fiber is perpendicular than when it is parallel to that plane.

As shown by the dotted lines just referred to, the deflection is upward until the shot has arrived at some point *C'* when the pressure on the lower portion of the shot has become less than it is on the upper portion. This must take place, since the lower part of the perforation is completed first, and the shot then meets with resistance on the upper side only. The last part of the perforation is done at a lower velocity than the first, and of course the deflection is correspondingly greater; and the final direction on leaving the plate is downward from the direction of impact, as before stated

The amount of the deflection is diminished by the bending of the plate, at first downward, and after the resistance begins to diminish it springs back As this motion of the plate tends to accommodate itself to the motion of the projectile, the effect is to diminish the amount of deviation of the latter from a straight line.

The amount of this deflection, for several particular cases, is shown by rounds 452 to 457 inclusive, Plate XIX. Also, for laminated targets, by rounds 462 and 463, same plate.

As to the concussion or shock produced, it may be remarked that the inclined plate again has the advantage, since the concussion varies directly with the velocity of impact, and this velocity, measured in the direction of the normal, is diminished as the angle of incidence increases, or is equal to the velocity of the shot multiplied by the cosine of the angle of incidence. While this is the case, it should also be borne in mind that no amount of ingenuity in providing lubricated, or elastic surfaces, friction balls, or other devices for deflecting the shot without injury to the plate, can evade the consequences of this law. A shot cannot be deflected from its course in any possible manner without delivering a blow to the deflecting medium, whatever it may be.

6

In fact, so far as the normal component is concerned, it would be better to allow a shot to "bite in" and stop than to deflect it, provided, of course, that the plate is thick enough to be safe from perforation. This will appear from a consideration of the laws of impact of bodies. When one perfectly *elastic* body strikes another, the motion imparted to it is double what it would be if the bodies were perfectly *inelastic*. From this extreme case we may conclude that any approach to elasticity in armor-plating is a step in the wrong direction.

The foregoing supposes the shot to be moving in a horizontal direction, but in case of an angle of arrival, as in the line $C'' f$, which is the more general case in practice, there is an advantage in favor of the vertical plate as compared with the inclined plate $A B'$; but the inclined plate $A B''$ would have a still greater advantage, as will be clearly seen by comparing the lengths of the portions of the line $C'' f$, cut out by the different plates. Where such a slope can be given to any portion of a defensive work, it will be by far the most efficient way in which a given surface can be covered.

The foregoing remarks, though requiring slight modification to suit the case of elongated projectiles, are essentially correct for any form of shot.

The additional circumstances which arise in case of rifle shot will now be considered.

Numerous experiments have been made in Europe with plates placed at an angle with the axis of the gun, but there seems to have been no attention paid to the angle between the axis of the shot and the trajectory at the point of impact.

This latter has a very important bearing upon the use of rifle projectiles at long range.

In Fig. 7, Plate XXI, a shot is supposed to have been fired at an elevation of 15° in order to strike a vertical target at considerable distance and on the same horizontal plane.

If the axis of this shot remains parallel to itself during its flight, it will arrive at the target making an angle of something more than thirty degrees with the trajectory, and if, under these circumstances, the shot gets through the plate, it must make a hole as large, at least, as the projection of the shot upon the plate by lines parallel to the trajectory at the point of impact. In the figure, the dotted lines A B and C D are the projecting lines of the vertical section, and the portion of the plate between them must be removed. The distance between these projecting lines will be, for small angles, about equal to the diameter of the shot, plus the length of the shot into the sine of the angle between the axis of the shot and the trajectory.

In this particular case, if we call the diameter of the shot one foot and its length two feet, the angle being 30° and its sine ½, we have for the length of the hole, perpendicular to the trajectory, $1' + 2' \times \frac{1}{2} = 2'$, and for the length of the hole on the surface this distance must be divided by the cosine of the angle of incidence.

But the work of punching, all other circumstances being equal, increases nearly with the circumference of the punch. It has, therefore, in this case, been nearly doubled.

The range for the 8-inch rifled gun at 15° elevation and 12.5 pounds charge is given at 4,435 yards, or about 2½ miles. Supposing that at the muzzle of the gun this shot could perforate an 8-inch plate, it would lose from resistance of the air so much of its velocity that at 2½ miles its power of penetration would be reduced to about 4 inches, and, from the above-mentioned cause, it would lose about one-half of this, and would probably be stopped by a 2½-inch plate.

From this it appears that the penetration of armor at long ranges must be very difficult at best, and it is not improbable that smooth-bored guns with spherical shot may answer better for this purpose than rifled guns and elongated projectiles, since the former would not be subject to these disadvantages.

The most perfect remedy, however, would be in a shot which would remain tangent to the trajectory instead of keeping parallel to itself, and this has been attempted in various ways, though the object in view has generally been to provide for the use of elongated projectiles in smooth-bored guns.

No device for this purpose has been pronounced satisfactory, though there appears to be no mechanical impossibility in the way; and it seems quite likely that the simple plan of placing the center of gravity in front of the center of figure of the projectile, may yet accomplish the desired result. I am aware that this plan has been tried, but at the same time am satisfied that the want of success was owing to the fact that the principle was not properly carried out, and not to any defect in the principle itself.

Another point in connection with oblique impact, is the effect of different forms of head upon the rotation of the shot after impact. If the axis of the shot is tangent to the trajectory on impact, and at the same time normal to the target, there will be no tendency to rotate about any axis parallel with the plane of the target.

In Fig. 5, Plate XXI, if we suppose a shot to arrive at *A* under these conditions, it will undoubtedly penetrate the plate directly. But let one arrive as at *D* or *E*, and there will be a tendency to rotate, and this tendency will depend upon the form of the shot as well as upon the angle between the trajectory and its axis.

The advantage in this latter case will be in favor of flat-headed shot, since the moment of the rotating force will be the variable resistance of the plate multiplied by the lever arm *D d*, for the pointed shot, and the same multiplied by a much shorter lever arm *E e*, in case of the flat-headed shot, and this may be negative; or, in other words, there may be a tendency to rotate toward the normal, which would be a decided advantage. This would take place when the line of the trajectory passed within the base of the shot.

In the third case, represented at *B* and *C*, a shot is moving with its axis tangent to the trajectory, but oblique to the target; here there is also a tendency for the flat-headed shot to rotate toward the normal, but it is questionable whether such rotation would be advantageous. The pointed or ogival shot would have a less tendency to such rotation, and in this, as in all the foregoing cases, the cylindro-spherical shot would occupy an intermediate position with reference to the cylindrical and ogival ones.

For the spherical shot the second case reduces to the third, and the first would be similar to that of the cylindro-spherical shot.

QUALITY OF METAL FOR ARMOR-PLATING.

In the use of large masses of metal for armor-plating it becomes a question of great importance to select from among numerous available varieties that which is, all things considered, best suited to the purpose.

The most obvious manner of accomplishing this would be to take specimen plates, from each kind of metal, and subject them to actual battering; and, accordingly, this method has been employed, to a considerable extent, both in Europe and in this country.

But considering the large number of grades of metal from which the selection must be made, differing perhaps slightly from each other, but each possessing its own peculiar advantages, and also the fact that it would require several specimens of each kind, especially of those possessing a near approach to the desired qualities, to give sufficient data for determining with accuracy their relative merits; it is evident that this method would involve a very long series of experiments, and that a less objectionable plan for even partially overcoming the difficulty, as, for example, by determining the quality of the metal, within certain known limits, and thus reducing the number of grades from which the selection must be made, would be of very great utility.

Turning to the physical properties of metals for an index to their fitness for the purpose, we find that it can be neither "hardness," "elasticity," nor "crushing strength," for cast iron possesses all these qualities in a higher degree than wrought iron, and yet is comparatively worthless for armor-plating. Copper, tin, and lead possess them in a lower degree, and are also unsuited to the purpose, or at least would require to be used in much greater thickness, than wrought iron.

It cannot be "density" nor "tensile strength," or hardened steel would be better than wrought iron, which is not the case. For similar reasons it is inferred that neither "ductility" nor "malleability" can of themselves indicate anything in regard to the subject of investigation.

If, however, we combine the *tensile strength* with the *ductility*, we may get an expression for the *work* of breaking the bar; and although the work of *punching* involves crushing and transverse resistances as well as tenacity, it may be shown that the *resistance* to impact depends to a very great extent upon the tensile strength of the metal, and that the space over which this resistance must be overcome depends chiefly upon the ductility or amount of distortion which the metal will endure before rupture takes place.

It should be here stated that the usual method of testing specimens of metal for tensile strength is believed to be entirely defective in principle, and only gives tolerably correct results in practice from accidental circumstances. What I refer to as the "usual" method is the breaking of specimens of the form shown in Fig. 2, Plate II, and assuming the strain required to break them as the measure of excellence of the metal, for purposes where tensile strains are to be resisted. The points in error are the following:

1st. The form of the specimen is such that unless the weakest point happens to occur at the smallest section of the specimen, the fractured area will be larger than the measured section of the specimen. It is no unusual thing to see a specimen of bronze, or cast iron, break where the section is fifty per cent. larger than that used in computing the tensile strength per square inch. By using the long cylindrical specimens this source of error will be avoided in all but a few exceptional cases, arising from flaws or other defects in the specimen.

2nd. The form of the specimen admits of transverse strains due to the unequal bearing of the ends of the specimen in the sockets of the testing machine. This defect would be greatly improved by using longer specimens as already proposed.

3rd. The simple measure of the strain required to break a piece of metal, without regard to the amount of elongation produced before rupture takes place, is not a measure of what occurs in practice, any more than the *length* of a piece of land is a proper criterion by which to compare it with another piece, of different form and breadth.

It is difficult to conceive of a bar of iron being broken without a certain space being passed over by the breaking force, in separating the fibers, and as this space bears no analogy whatever to the tensile strength of the metal, it must come in as an independent factor. For example, the metal of a cannon is stretched at every discharge; the tie-rods, struts, and girders of a railroad bridge are elongated or compressed every time a train passes; and, in fact, wherever metal is subject to a variable strain, there must be a corresponding change of length. These elongations may be very small in amount—so small, in fact, as to be inappreciable in ordinary measurements; but it is no less certain that they exist.

In these, as in all other cases, where an elongation is to be repeatedly sustained, the strain must evidently be kept within the elastic limits; but where a structure is to sustain but one, or at most a very limited number of strains, as in case of an armor-plate or a projectile, the elastic limits may be disregarded. It is also evident that the efficiency of a piece of metal, in counteracting a strain, must depend upon whether most of the elongation takes place before the strain has reached a considerable intensity, or whether it takes place after that time. In other words, the *relation* between the strain and the elongation produced by it is an essential element.

In order to apply these principles in testing several kinds of iron and steel, specimens were cut from the plates with a planing machine and turned down to fit the sockets of a testing machine, as represented in Fig. 4, Plate I, some of these specimens being cut lengthwise, some diagonally, and some crosswise the plates. In testing armor-plates they could be cut from that portion cut out to form the embrasure. A convenient size for these specimens would be one inch in diameter and one foot long in the cylindrical part. Those tested in these experiments have been generally half an inch in diameter and from seven to nine inches long.

These specimens were then placed in the testing machine and a steady strain applied, the middle portion of the specimen or that to be stretched being previously marked off in inches to afford the means of measuring the elongation. When the marked portion of the bar had been stretched a certain distance, say one-hundredth of its original length, the strain was recorded, and so on for equal increments of elongation until rupture took place.

This operation will be readily understood from a few examples illustrated by the diagrams Figs. 5 and 6, Plate XXIV. The abscissas represent the per cent. of elongation, and the ordinates the corresponding tensile strain in pounds. The area inclosed by the curve, the axis of x, and the extreme ordinate, represents the work of breaking the specimen, as before mentioned. Although this method gave very satisfactory results, it involved too much time and trouble in measuring, recording, and plotting the result; and to avoid this, as well as to secure a continuous record in a more direct manner, the indicator, Fig. 1, Plate II, described on page 12 was devised. The working of this instrument was all that could have been anticipated, and it should (with some slight modification of details) form an essential part of all testing apparatus for tensile strength of materials, whatever may be the use for which such materials are designed.

The mode of testing the specimens with this instrument, and of treating the results, was as follows: The specimen having been placed in the testing machine and the indicator attached, the cylinder having been previously covered with letter paper, the pencil was adjusted and the power applied to the machine. The addition of weight revolved the cylinder and the elongation of the specimen moved the pencil point as already described, and a continuous curve was marked upon the paper until the rupture of the specimen took place. The co-ordinate axes of the curve were then marked by revolving the cylinder while the pencil was stationary, and by sliding the pencil while the cylinder was stationary, as shown on the engraving of the instrument already referred to. After as many specimens had been recorded in this way as the cylinder would hold, the paper was cut, parallel to the axis of the cylinder and placed upon a drawing board for the purpose of measuring the areas of the curves.

This was done with Amsler's planimeter already mentioned, (page 13,) the operation being repeated several times and the *mean* result taken. The probable error was thus easily reduced to less than the smallest measure of the testing machine, which was of course accurate enough for all purposes. This gave the work of breaking the specimen, but the ordinates of the curve, which were one dimension of the area measured, represented pounds, and in order to reduce them to that unit it was necessary to multiply by the number of pounds to the inch, which in this case was 5,000. This gave the work in foot-pounds, and it was only necessary to divide by the length and area of section of the specimen to reduce the result to a standard specimen one foot long and one inch area of section.

The following points were found desirable in preparing specimens:

1st. The specimens should be cut from the plates with a planing, or slotting machine, and great care should be taken not to bend, hammer, or otherwise strain the metal during the operation. They should then be turned accurately to a cylindrical form and a diameter slightly larger than that required for the finished specimens; after which they should be draw-filed to the exact size, thus removing tool marks and giving a smooth surface.

2nd. Specimens from different qualities of metal should be as nearly of the same length and diameter as practicable. It cannot be asserted, from experiments heretofore made, that this requirement is essential; but in the absence of positive information to the contrary, it will be best to observe it. The results of these experiments, so far as they bear upon the subject, indicate that the shorter specimens give the greater per cent of elongation, and this is what might be expected, since the shorter the specimen the fewer the chances of flaws or cracks.

3rd. The junction of the cylindrical portion of the specimen with the knob or head should be by a gradual enlargement, and the head should be no larger than is required to resist the tendency to pull through the sockets. For this purpose it was found that a very small enlargement would suffice. In fact there was no instance, in testing more than a hundred specimens, of the head drawing through, although in many cases the shoulder or bearing surface was very much smaller than the fractured section of the specimen.

4th. The measured portion of the specimen should be marked with a sharp center-punch. If marked with a cold-chisel or a file the specimen is almost certain to break at that point, which is not the case when the center punch is used, as the latter seems to separate instead of cutting the fibers.

5th. Much labor in turning out specimens may be saved by the use of sockets with conical wedges, (Figs. 1 and 2, Plate XXVII,) which were devised for the purpose of taking hold of the middle portion of broken specimens and breaking them a second time. It will be seen that by cutting out the specimen barely large enough to turn up to the required diameter, a great saving may be effected over the usual method, which requires the ends of the specimen to be quite large, while the middle portion, for nearly the whole length of the specimen, has to be turned down to a much smaller diameter.

6th. In testing specimens, the strain should be applied steadily and continuously until rupture takes place.

7th. Quite a number of specimens of each kind should be tested under as nearly identical circumstances as practicable, in order to get reliable mean results.

8th. An equal number of specimens should be cut lengthwise and crosswise the plate, and where this is not done, the specimens cut in each direction should be kept by themselves and the mean of each kind should be taken separately. The proper mode of combining these results has not been definitely ascertained, but it appears, for certain reasons, most proper to take the diagonal of the rectangle formed by them—that is, the square root of the sum of their squares.

9th. In the measure of quality of metal to be subjected to repeated strains, only that portion of the area of the curve between the initial point and the ordinate through the elastic limit, must be included, but where the strain is not to be repeated, the whole area of the curve must be taken.

The following are some of the more important results obtained in testing specimens in this manner:

1st. The first part of the elongation gives a very slight curve, which shows that the elongation increases rather more rapidly than the strain upon the specimen. This part of the curve extends from the origin to the point *a*, Figs. 5 and 6, Plate XXIV.

2nd. At the point *a*, which is about five-eighths of the breaking weight, as shown by taking the mean of a large number of results, the specimen begins to elongate freely, and there is a well-defined change in the rate of increase. The point *a* probably coincides with the elastic limit.

3rd. The strain increases, as the elongation continues, almost up to the breaking point *b*. This shows that the tenacity of metal which has been stretched beyond the elastic limit, is not entirely destroyed, as is commonly believed, but that the work of rupture has but just commenced.

4th. Just before rupture takes place, in case of good iron, the specimen is observed to suddenly contract at some point, sometimes at two, and very rarely at a greater number of points, the strain slightly diminishing at the generally with a sudden snap, though very soft iron sometimes breaks so quietly as not to be heard at all. Steel, on the other hand, breaks with a report nearly as loud as that of a small pistol.

5th. The effect of the elongation of specimens in this manner is to change the smooth surface of the specimen to a rough and scaly appearance; and in case of gun metal, (bronze,) the specimen becomes so irregular as to resemble a roll of putty flattened in various directions between the thumb and finger. (Fig. 1, Plate XXVII.) The elongation of steel develops innumerable fine cracks nearly perpendicular to the surface.

6th. In breaking a specimen a second or third time, it would seem that the metal must get weaker, especially since the sudden breaking produces a violent shock, but such is not the case, as will be seen from the following table:

TABLE II.

No. of specimen.	Kind of metal.	Breaking strain. (In pounds.)		Per cent. of increase in breaking strain.	Elongation. (Per cent.)	
		1st time.	2nd time.		1st time.	2nd time.
17	Wrought iron	44,580	56,100	.28	18.75	Not measured.
18	Wrought iron	42,585	51,000	19	132	Not measured.
22	Wrought iron	46,920	56,100	.19	18	Not measured.
61	Wrought iron	51,410	54,000	.008	26	Not measured.
			*54,570	.06	-	Not measured.
40	Wrought iron	48,720	51,000	.047	167	Not measured.
42	Wrought iron	42,130	51,000	.18	.115	Not measured.
49	Bessemer steel, (rolled,)	82,990	96,970	.167	.104	.0024.
50	Bessemer steel, (rolled,)	80,448	81,600	.014	.063	.0007.
52	Bessemer steel, (rolled,)	77,393	87,700	.13	.054	Not measured.
			*87,700			
54	Bessemer steel, (rolled,)	81,460	84,640	.038	.125	.016.
13	Bessemer steel, (cast,)	65,000	64,000	.0	.049	Not measured.
16	Bessemer steel, (cast.)	72,000	80,835	.12	.068	Not measured.
	Gun-metal	36,210	38,250	.056	.364	Not measured.
1	Wrought iron	54,442	56,100	.03	24	Not measured.
			*63,393	.17	. .	Not measured.

* Third time of breaking.

On the contrary, the specimen evidently breaks at the weakest point, and the shock and previous stretching have not been sufficient to reduce the strength of the next weakest part of the specimen below that of the first one. It was found that even the third breaking required a greater strain than the second. Of course, the *work* of breaking was greatly diminished each time, but in one case the work of breaking a specimen the second time was almost equal to that of the first breaking.

7th. The uniformity of the specimen is as important as the quality of metal in increasing the work of breaking. To take an extreme case: Suppose one part of a specimen to be more than one and three-fifths times as strong, statically, as another. From what has preceded, it is evident that this stronger portion will not be perceptibly elongated, for before it has passed its elastic limit the weaker portion will have reached its breaking point. It will not, therefore, contribute to increase the elongation, and since the specimen can be no stronger than its weakest part it must diminish the work of breaking the specimen just in the proportion that its length bears to the whole length of the specimen. In other words, increasing the strength of one portion of a specimen, or of a structure, may diminish the dynamical strength of the whole structure.

The practical importance of this principle is apparent, especially in structures which, like armor-plating, depend upon dynamical resistance. Every part of such a structure which can be made so, should be a "solid of equal resistance." The great difficulty will, of course, be to ascertain where and how the strains are to be applied, since such structures are liable to be struck at an indefinite number of points; but the strains upon certain parts may, from their relation to the rest of the structure, be determined with sufficient accuracy to show what form these parts should have. Among these may be classed bolts, girders, and struts.

8th. Good plate iron gives an elongation, lengthwise the fiber, of fifteen to twenty-five per cent., and crosswise from eight to twelve per cent. The elongation given by specimens cut diagonally is generally intermediate.

9th. Hammered plates, and those which have been most thoroughly worked before rolling, show greater uniformity of results than those which have been simply rolled. Specimens cut crosswise a plate of such iron often give nearly as good results as those cut lengthwise.

The following varieties of iron and steel were procured and tested in accordance with these principles:

The first nine sets of plates were procured under direction of Colonel J. N. Macomb, U. S. Engineers, by Mr. E. M. Shield, who also furnished the following brief account of their manufacture:

1. "Plates marked V, are from the Laclede Works of Chouteau, Harrison & Vallee, St. Louis, Missouri. Iron Mountain ore smelted with and made into pig metal with charcoal, cold blast. From pig metal puddled into balls with bituminous coal from Illinois. Hammered and reheated previous to rolling. In these various stages of conversion the same bituminous coal named was used.

"This bituminous coal is highly impregnated with sulphur, and its use in the conversion from pig metal to bloom must deteriorate the quality of the original iron.

2. "Plates marked VV, are from the works of Phillips & Son, Covington, Kentucky, were manufactured from Tennessee blooms, made with charcoal, reheated with bituminous coal from Pittsburg, Pennsylvania, and rolled.

3. "Plates marked VVV, were manufactured at the Swift Iron Works, Alex. Swift & Company, Newport, Kentucky. Tennessee ore, smelted with charcoal, and run into pig metal, cold blast. Pig metal worked in a knobbling fire fed with charcoal, and the balls hammered into blooms: blooms reheated with bituminous coal from Steubenville, Ohio, and rehammered: reheated with same coal, and rolled.

"The bituminous coal has a high standard of excellence for reheating iron.

4. "Plates marked VVVV, were manufactured by Hillman Brothers, Nashville, Tennessee, at their works on Cumberland River, from Tennessee ore, smelted with charcoal, cold blast. Pig metal knobbed in a charcoal forge; balls hammered into blooms, with Pittsburg bituminous coal, and rolled into plates.

5. "Plates marked 1, from the manufactory of Brown & Company, Wayne Iron and Steel Works, Pittsburg, Pennsylvania; from Tennessee ore, smelted with and run into pig metal with charcoal, cold blast. Pig metal converted

into blooms with charcoal: blooms reheated with bituminous coal from the Monongahela mines, and hammered into plates.

"The character of the bituminous coal is too well known to require any explanation of its quality for this work.

6. "Plates marked 2, were made from blooms manufactured at the celebrated Cumberland Iron Works, Tennessee. This iron is made wholly with charcoal, and bears a high character for its softness and pliability: the plates made from this iron are double hammered.

7. "Plates marked 3, were from cold-blast iron, smelted with charcoal: converted into blooms with bituminous coal from the Monongahela River; reheated with same coal, and hammered into plates.

8. "Plates marked 4, from a mixture of ores, smelted with bituminous coal, cold blast; converted into blooms with bituminous coal; hammered; reheated with same coal, and rolled.

9. "Plates marked 5, from charcoal cold blast: Hanging Rock, Ohio. Pig metal smelted with charcoal: converted into blooms by puddling; bituminous coal used: blooms double worked and hammered; reheated, and rolled.

"These five latter series of plates are all from the Wayne Iron and Steel Works of Brown & Company, Pittsburg, Pennsylvania."

* * * * * * * *

The four following varieties were furnished by Messrs. Moorhead & Company, Pittsburg, Pennsylvania.

10. Plates marked X, were from Lake Superior charcoal pig iron, refined and puddled.

11. Plates marked XX, same pig iron, but not put through the refinery.

12. Plates marked XXX, Juniata pig, treated like that last mentioned.

13. Plates marked XXXX, common puddled iron.

14. Common plate-iron from Washington navy yard, of the quality used for gun-carriages, &c

15. Cast iron, cut from plates one inch thick and one foot square.

16. Plates cut from a fragment of one of the 12 by 15-inch hammered beams in the experimental casemate at Fort Monroe, Virginia; manufactured by Moorhead & Company, Pittsburg, Pennsylvania. Three-fourths Lake

instant, and when the power is still further applied the specimen breaks, Superior charcoal, and one-fourth Juniata; forged with a four-ton hammer.

17. Plates cut from a 12-inch plate from the same structure; same as beams, excepting that it was rolled instead of hammered.

18. Bessemer steel, rolled; manufactured at the works of John A. Griswold & Company, Troy, New York.

19. Bessemer steel, cut from cylindrical ingots twelve inches in diameter and two feet long. Made at the same establishment.

20. Gun-metal or bronze: an alloy of ninety parts copper, ten of tin, and two of zinc. Made at the Washington navy yard.

The following table gives the results of testing the foregoing specimens:

TABLE III.

No.	Mark.	Work. (In foot-pounds.)		
		Lengthwise.	Diagonal.	Crosswise.
1	V	[illegible]	1760.	[illegible]
2	VV	[illegible]	3355.	[illegible]
3	VVV	[illegible]	[illegible]	6203.5
4	VVVV	[illegible]	[illegible]	5435.
5	1	[illegible].5	[illegible]	[illegible]
6	2	4584.5	[illegible].5	[illegible].5
7	3	9530.	5713.5	[illegible]
8	4	[illegible]	[illegible]	[illegible].5
9	5	[illegible]	[illegible]	[illegible]
10	X	[illegible]	[illegible]	5417.
11	XX	5415.	1720.	1785.
12	XXX	4066.	1501.	1078.
13	XXXX	3980.	1430.	1144.
14	Common iron from navy yard	*3069.		*1024
15	Cast iron	98.		
16	Fort Monroe, (beams)	5266.		
17	Fort Monroe, (plate)	2032.		
18	Bessemer steel, (rolled)	7335.		
19	Bessemer steel, (cast)	*3543.		
20	Gun-metal, (bronze)	12640.		

* These results were deduced from the tensile strength and extreme elongation.

It has for some years been the practice in England, and to a limited extent in this country, to measure the elongation in connection with the tensile strain. But instead of computing the actual quantity of work, it seems to have been considered sufficient to simply multiply the breaking weight by the extreme elongation per unit of length.

Comparing this method with the foregoing, it was found that the results were from five to twenty-five per cent greater, and, by rejecting certain specimens, it was found that a mean value of fifteen per cent had a probable error of .008.

An allowance of fifteen per cent will, therefore, give an approximate correction for reducing results obtained by the English method, to the same standard as those in the foregoing table, and thus furnish a means of comparing our metals with those of other countries.

The following table gives the results of some specimens, tested at the Royal Gun Factories at Woolwich, to which this reduction has been applied.

It should be stated that the specimens from which these results were obtained were only 2 inches in length, and this may have affected the results as compared with those in the foregoing table, which were in no case less than 6 inches long.

TABLE IV.

Specimens of wrought iron, tested at the Royal Gun Factories, Woolwich.

(Reduced to the standard of the foregoing table.)

Kind of metal.	Work in foot pounds.	No. of specimens from which mean is taken.
[illegible]-inch rolled plate from Atlas Works	9,148	[illegible]
[illegible]-inch hammered plate, from Thames Works	10,220	6
Exterior plate, Plymouth target	8,479	3
[illegible]-inch plank, (same)	[illegible]	4
Inner plate, below port, (same)	6,2[illegible]	3
Exterior plate, experimental casemate, ("War Office Shield.")	10,[illegible]	2
Petin, Gaudet & Co., [illegible] and [illegible]-inch plates	[illegible]	6
Millwall [illegible]-inch plates	7,442	3
Cammell's [illegible] and [illegible]-inch plates	5,732	2

Finally the questions arise, How far does the measure thus found represent the quality of metal for armor-plating, and in what manner must it be employed?

In the first place, like all similar measures, it is only relative, or a means of comparison between similar properties of the metal.

Secondly. It is only a partial measure, since other properties affect the efficiency of metal in stopping projectiles; of these only two will be mentioned, viz: inertia and hardness.

It is evident that inertia must exercise considerable influence independently of the dynamical measure in question, since a pile of sand or of any other heavy material, without the slightest amount of ductility, may stop a projectile. To get an idea of the importance of this consideration, suppose a plate one foot thick to be made up of cubes of cast iron or steel, indefinitely small but fitting closely together and forming a solid mass, entirely destitute of ductility and tensile strength. A shot of the same material, one foot long and cylindrical in form, would, on striking such a target at right angles, impart motion to its own volume, and consequently its own weight of the material of the target, and in doing so would lose at least one-half of its own velocity and a corresponding portion of its work, the latter being expended in crushing the material; and its amount depending upon the elasticity and density of the metal.

The foregoing measure for quality must, therefore, be increased by an independent term which, for the present, we must consider a constant for those qualities of iron usually employed in armor-plating, though it doubtless increases with the specific gravity of the metal, and with the thickness of plate required to stop a projectile. That is, $P = a + u$ . . . . (7) where P = the quality or efficiency of the metal to resist impact: a = a constant, and u = the dynamical measure already described.

Thirdly. In regard to hardness, it will be recollected that in the discussion of the subject of impact of projectiles, it was held that penetration and concussion are to a certain extent complementary or alternative effects, one increasing as the other diminishes. It will now appear that the foregoing measure must relate more to the latter than to the former of these effects,

8

and that where the former is more particularly considered, another quality must be taken into account, viz: hardness or resistance to indentation.

In a few experiments upon this quality the indenting tools represented, Figs 3 and 4, Plate XXVII, and described among the other apparatus, were used. The depth of the indentation was measured for successive increments of pressure upon the indenting tool; and the work of producing an indent, of a given depth, was thus arrived at in a manner entirely analogous to that already described, for measuring the work of punching a shot through a plate. The metals tested were some of those to which the other tests were applied, and were marked as described page 53.

The results recorded in the following table were produced with the triangular form of indenting tool, the figures in the second column representing the number of foot-pounds of work required to make an indent with that tool three-eighths of an inch deep, by a steady pressure.

TABLE V.

Mark of specimen.	Work of making an indent ⅜ inch deep.
1	199 foot-pounds.
2	314 foot-pounds.
3	300 foot-pounds.
4	263 foot-pounds.
5	189 foot-pounds.
V	268 foot-pounds.
VV	245 foot-pounds.
VVV	232 foot-pounds.
VVVV	216 foot-pounds.
X	300 foot-pounds.
XX	207 foot-pounds.
XXX	229 foot-pounds.
XXXX	252 foot-pounds.
Gun-metal (bronze)	166 foot-pounds.
Copper	154 foot-pounds.

By comparing this table with Table III, page 55, it will be seen that the results in the two cases are entirely independent of each other, and that it may become necessary in some cases to sacrifice one of these qualities to secure the other. Thus, gun-metal gives the greatest dynamical measure, whereas it gives the least resistance to penetration; a fact which was corroborated by firing at specimens of the same metal.

It may be safely assumed that for thick iron or steel plates, and probably for all plates likely to be used in service, it will be found best to neglect this quality where it is obtained at the expense of the ductility, and it may be advisable in some cases to consider it as a negative quality. In almost all cases, if an iron or steel plate is thick enough to resist breaking or cracking, it will be thick enough to resist perforation; but if it is desired to employ the softer metals, as lead, copper, or any of their compounds, it will be necessary to consider their hardness.

As far as these principles have been verified the results accord with those obtained by firing, though it should be stated that this does not indicate that the elongation of the metal, under a sudden strain, like that produced by the impact of a shot, is the same as that due to the gradual application of force in the testing machine. On the contrary, it is well known that the more suddenly the strain is applied, the less ductility will be developed: and the utility of the foregoing measure for the quality of metal, only requires that the amounts of ductility developed in different specimens should be greater for those which give the greater *elongation* in the testing machine, however much their *absolute* values may be varied, by changing the rate of application of the rupturing force

Economy of Plating.

Another question which naturally comes in at this point is the relative cost of the different kinds of metal. If two kinds of metal are equally good, of course the cheaper is to be preferred: but where the qualities are also different, what weight is to be given to the difference of cost in deciding between them?

Let (A) represent a given sum to be expended in plating a given surface, a. $\frac{A}{a}$ will then be the cost of plating a unit of surface, say one square foot. If, now, c is the cost per cubic foot of the metal, $\frac{A}{a} \div c$, or $\frac{A}{ac}$, will be the thickness of metal which can be obtained for the given sum of money.

But, other circumstances being equal, the protection afforded by plating increases nearly with the square of the thickness, or $\left(\frac{A}{a\,c}\right)^2$, and since, by hypothesis, A and a are constant, the efficiency of the plating will vary inversely as c^2, or, combining this with the foregoing expression for *quality* of metal, we have—

$$Q = \frac{P}{c^2} \quad \ldots\ldots\ldots\ldots\ldots\ldots\ldots\ldots\ldots\ldots (8)$$

in which Q = what we may call the "coefficient of economy" of the metal;

P = the measure of quality of the metal; and

c = the cost of metal per cubic foot.

The foregoing computation is made on the supposition that the qualities and costs of metal differ so slightly from each other that the law of the square of the thickness is sufficiently accurate; but where this is not the case, recourse must be had to equation 4, page 30, from which a more accurate result may be readily computed.

Lest it should be thought that the question of economy has been kept too prominently in view in this report, it may be stated that it is *the* question upon which the use of armor plating, in connection with our permanent works, must depend. That iron casemates are practicable, no one can doubt, and their construction, independent of expense, would require no further ingenuity than to replace the blocks of granite in the scarp walls of our present works by blocks of wrought iron properly doweled together. This is merely proposed to show how simple the problem would become were it possible to omit the *cost* from the calculation.

SOLID PLATING.

The solid plate—a plate in which the whole material is in a single thickness—is at once the most simple and natural one to serve as a standard of comparison, as well as for the general purposes of experiments, where no special form or combination is called for. It therefore holds the first place in this series of experiments.

As a standard of comparison, it was used to measure the value of laminated plating, Bessemer steel, lead concrete, and various other materials, and of several forms of compound targets.

For general purposes, it was chiefly used in determining the relative penetrating power of projectiles of various forms, the relation between thickness of plate and work of perforation, and the laws of oblique impact. Each of these subjects will be discussed under its own heading, and nearly all that relates to solid plating will, therefore, be given in connection with these collateral branches.

Some of the results of firing at solid plates are shown on plates VI and VII. (Front and back.)

From these results, and, in fact, from all that can be gathered in relation to the subject, it appears that if a solid plate of such dimensions as to stop all projectiles could be made at reasonable cost, it would settle the whole question of armor at once, so far, at least, as land defenses are concerned.

But, in addition to sufficient thickness, there must be sufficient superficial area to cover a gun or the front of a casemate; and if this area cannot be provided in a single plate, it must be made up by joining two or more plates edge to edge, thus leading to the difficulty of covering and strengthening joints.*

In fact, it has been found that for want of suitable furnaces for heating and machinery for handling and rolling such enormous masses of metal, fifteen inches is the greatest thickness of plate that can be made up to the present time, and this was only attained by reducing the width of the plate to only four feet. This thickness is about sufficient to stop all known projectiles, but the width is not sufficient to resist the traverse strain, and plates of this description will consequently be broken across instead of perforated, as was the case at Shoeburyness.

We may, therefore, conclude that until heavier plant is introduced into our rolling mills, solid plating will be impracticable.

Whatever may be the relative cost of heavy and light masses of iron at some future time, it is certain that at present the cost of heavy plating is

* NOTE.—Since the foregoing was written, it has been announced that 5-inch plates, large enough to cover the front of a casemate, have been made in England by rolling the pile both lengthwise and crosswise; and a shield formed of three such plates, separated by 5-inch layers of "tar concrete," has been tested with good results at Shoeburyness.

largely in excess, both from the fact that it costs more to make it in the first instance, and because a failure in any case from a defective weld, or other cause, subjects the manufacturer to heavy loss from having a large mass of metal in a form difficult to treat.

We come, then, from necessity, rather than from choice, to the subject of laminated plating.

LAMINATED PLATING.

At the time these experiments were commenced, one of the most unsettled questions in connection with the use of iron for defensive purposes was the relative advantages of solid and laminated armor.

The experiments in this direction had not been numerous, and the conclusion seemed to have been arrived at, that solid plating was so far superior to laminated, that it was not worth while to seek for a comparison between them.

Holley, in his most excellent work on Ordnance and Armor, gives the strength of laminated armor as varying with the sum of the squares of the thicknesses of the plates of which it is composed. This would make twelve plates of one inch thickness each but one-twelfth as strong as a single plate twelve inches thick, or $12\ (1)^2 = \frac{1}{12}\ (12)^2$.

Captain Noble, in his report on experiments carried out by the ordnance select committee, says, "This description of iron plating has been extensively used in America on account of its cheapness and facility of construction; it, however, offers much less resistance to shot than solid plating." Also, conclusions, Table XI, same report:

1st. That "laminated armor is considerably weaker than solid armor. Thus a 4-inch solid plate would have effectually stopped all the projectiles, whereas they easily penetrated six inches of laminated plates."

2nd. "The experiments are not sufficiently numerous or extensive to warrant a comparison being made between the relative resistances of solid and laminated armor."

The statement that the shot which penetrated the 6-inch target would have been stopped by a 4-inch solid plate, seems doubtful from the data given. Three shots only went through the target, two of which struck with a work of 45.7 foot-tons per inch of circumference, and one with 35.3 foot tons. The first two would have gone through 5½ inches and the last through 5 inches of solid metal, according to Table X of the same report.

These facts are mentioned to show the views entertained on this subject as late as 1866, and after millions of dollars had been expended on experiments in various parts of the world.

In order to test these statements numerous experiments were made with laminated targets, made up of plates from ⅛ to ½-inch thick, and from two to twelve in number. Each of these targets was subjected to the same firing tests as a corresponding single-plate target of the same thickness. Some of these targets are represented on Plates IX and X.

That at the top of Plate VIII was made by planing down and halving together two pieces of plate, in such a manner as to leave one portion ¾-inch thick, while another portion was made of two plates ⅜-inch thick each, the whole being of the same quality of iron, since the whole target was cut from the same plate. The result was decidedly in favor of the two thicknesses. It will be noticed that the shot were all cylindrical ones in these four rounds, viz: 411, 412, 423, and 424. Similar targets were fired at with cylindro-spherical and ogival shot, with similar results, though not as decidedly in favor of the two plates. Plate IX shows like results for the spherical shot, and Plate X represents two targets, made up of six and seven ⅛-inch plates, fired at with cylindrical, cylindro-spherical, and ogival shot.

In presenting the following conclusions, drawn from these experiments, it should be stated that the subject of laminated plating involves so many practical questions, besides the simple question of number and thickness of plates, that a final judgment upon its merits should be reserved until the more important of these collateral questions have been considered. Among the subjects which should thus be taken into account are the quality of metal, bolts, and other fastenings, backing, and even the form of the shield or casemate to be constructed.

Conclusions.—1st. Two plates in contact are so nearly equal to a single plate of their combined thickness, in regard to work of perforation, that a very slight difference in quality of metal, or other circumstances, will turn the scale of comparison between them.

2nd. As the number of plates to make up a given thickness increases, the work of perforating the combined mass diminishes very slightly, but up to six plates, compared with one, the difference is more than made up by the addition of another thin plate. For example, six plates, $\frac{1}{8}$-inch thick each, are not quite equal to one $\frac{3}{4}$-inch plate, but seven of the thinner plates are better. As laminated armor is much cheaper than solid, a fair comparison would be between equal values of metal covering a given surface; and this would doubtless give results decidedly in favor of two or more thicknesses.

3rd. The work of punching laminated plates is made up less by resistance, and more by distance passed over, than in case of solid plating. In other words, the shot is stopped more gradually and with less shock.

4th. In case of low velocities and very thin plates, the shot gets through by *tearing* rather than by punching.

5th. A target composed of plates of different thicknesses will offer a greater resistance when the thicker plates are placed *in rear* than when they are in front, as is generally the case.

6th. The superiority of solid plating over laminated is more manifest with the pointed forms of shot than with the flat-headed ones; in fact, it has been shown that in case of the perfectly flat-headed, cylindrical shot, two plates were actually better than one. The reason for this is that the flat-headed shot is converted at once into an iron-headed one, with a round, instead of sharp edge, by the piece cut out of the first plate in the laminated target, (see Plate V:) whereas the pointed shot has a better chance to force the metal out of the way laterally in the laminated, than in the solid target.

7th. A point in favor of solid plating is its greater power to break up, or *upset* the shot: in other words, to expend the work of the shot upon the shot itself.

8th. Another advantage gained by solid plating is that the number of bolts required to hold them in position is less than for laminated plating.

9th. It appears to make but little difference whether laminated plates are in absolute contact or slightly separated. This point will be further explained under the head of "Separated Plates."

And, finally, while it is evident that very thin plates cannot give as good results as a single plate of the same total thickness, it is by no means improbable that two, or even three thicknesses, may be economically substituted for the single one, especially since it has been found that the latter must be of such enormous thickness as to greatly increase the cost of rolling and fitting up.

It is also probable that a single heavy plate, say six or eight inches thick, reinforced *in front* by a sufficient number of thin plates, one or two inches thick each, to make up the required thickness, may be an equally or perhaps more advantageous combination.

In corroboration of these conclusions, it may be mentioned that, according to unofficial statements, it has been found at Shoeburyness, since these experiments were made, that the work of perforating one 7-inch plate, two 3½-inch, and three 2⅓-inch plates, is about as 15½, 14, and 13, respectively; these numbers representing the weight of the charges of powder required to send a 9-inch Palliser shot through each combination. More recently it is reported that a 10-inch plate has been perforated by a shot which had been stopped repeatedly by two 5-inch plates, though when the 5-inch plates were made of an inferior quality of iron they were also perforated by the same shot. It thus appears that the quality of the iron is of much greater importance than the number of plates employed to make a given thickness.

On the other hand, the reverse of these conclusions sometimes appears to obtain in case of targets composed of thin plates upon wooden backing, which have been tested both in this country and in Europe.

It is believed, however, that the demolition of these targets has chiefly resulted from the shot and pieces of the plate tearing through the backing, and from the numerous bolts which have been used, and that if these targets had been made thick enough to stop the shot before it reached the backing, the result would have been entirely different.

One point in explanation of this is worthy of notice. By far the greater number of experiments which have been made with armor-plating in this country and in Europe, were made with a view to the requirements of *floating* batteries, and but little attention has been given to the distinct wants of permanent defenses.

For naval purposes it is of great importance to avoid weight of metal, while for land defense this weight in itself is a decided advantage. A wooden backing is almost indispensable in the first case, and it is equally important to dispense with it in the latter. The monitor turrets are, perhaps, an exception to this last rule, but not to the former.

The consequence of all this has been, that experiments for testing the relative merits of solid and laminated armor have been made with targets built up of small pieces of timber, metal, bolts, washers, nuts, &c., in a manner especially adapted to produce a great splintering effect and wreck generally.

It would appear that the principles upon which these targets have been constructed are entirely wrong, and, as a rule, that they would offer a much greater resistance if turned around or fired at from the rear. As at present arranged, the density and solidity of the mass diminishes from front to rear. The front portion of the target is not, therefore, strengthened by being forced back upon the portion in rear; but the latter being lighter and less inert, is moved quicker and thus torn from the former as the shot passes through. On the other hand, let a shot strike the rear and lighter portion of the target and a great amount of work is expended in compressing this material against the heavier portions, which are last to move; and the work thus expended is absolute gain in the final result.

In illustration of this may be mentioned an experiment with a ⅜-inch plate and a 1⅛-inch oak plank. Placing the plank in front of the plate the combination stopped a shot which would have made a clean hole through a ¾-inch plate, and sometimes through ⅝-inch: or, the wood nearly doubled the work of perforation. But it is well known that a thin wooden *backing* does not materially increase the work of perforation, as was verified by placing the plank in rear of the iron.

The work absorbed in the first instance was that expended in compressing the 1⅛-inch plank into a thin lenticular piece, as shown in Fig. 1, Plate IV, this piece being almost as hard as the iron itself and firmly adhering to it. The shot, as seen in the figure, was cylindrical and flat-headed, which was, of course, favorable to this experiment; but the spherical and ogival ones gave similar results, only that the work absorbed was less in quantity and was given up in compressing the wood laterally as well as against the plate.

SEPARATED PLATES.

In the experiments with laminated plates, it was noticed that, when but slightly separated, the work of perforation was not materially reduced, and, in some cases, perhaps slightly increased; and a similar fact was noticed by Captain Inglis, royal engineers, in some of the experiments at Shoeburyness.

To test this point, several small targets were made of thin plates placed at various distances apart, from zero, or absolute contact, up to one inch, which last was found sufficient to prevent the plates from assisting each other perceptibly during the penetration. Some of the results are shown on Plate XI, (front and rear.)

Conclusions.—1st. A slight separation of the plates, depending upon their size and thickness, will not materially reduce the work of perforation.

2nd. Any considerable separation, depending upon the same conditions, will give a corresponding reduction of resisting power, this reduction increasing with the amount of separation until the plates are so far apart as to be perforated without being brought in contact.

3rd. The fragments punched out of the plates first struck, act as hindrances in punching the other plates. This is especially the case with flat-headed shot, which are converted into iron-headed ones, with round, instead of sharp, cutting edges. The effect of these fragments is less for the more pointed forms of shot, as they have a tendency to disperse them laterally instead of carrying them directly to the front, as is done by the flat-headed shot.

4th. When the plates were separated by such intervals as to make them practically independent of each other, the results showed conclusively that the supposed law of penetration—"that the work of perforation, other circumstances being equal, varies with the *square* of the thickness of the plate"—is inaccurate. For example: a spherical shot, fired with a charge of 300 grains, will be just stopped by $\frac{1}{2}$-inch of good iron. According to the rule just given this shot should almost perforate sixteen $\frac{1}{8}$-inch plates in succession, since $(\frac{1}{2})^2 = \frac{1}{4}$ and $(\frac{1}{8})^2 = \frac{1}{64}$, which is one-sixteenth of the former. But the result of actual experiment was that the shot went *through* only three, although there was a small hole through the fourth, and a slight indent in the fifth. Making all due allowance for the retarding effect of the fragments of plate, this shot could not have perforated more than five of these thin plates, or about one-third of the number called for by the rule. Again: the same shot should have perforated four ¼-inch plates, since $(\frac{1}{4})^2 \times 4 = (\frac{1}{2})^2$: whereas it only went through two, and, with the greatest allowance that could reasonably be made for the effect of fragments, it could not have gone through two and a half plates. In the same manner it was found that the ogival shot, which, with a 300-grain charge, would just perforate a ⅝-inch plate, should have perforated six and a quarter plates ¼-inch thick, according to the rule. In practice it went entirely through but three, while the point of the shot was barely through the fourth plate. These results are again referred to in deducing a formula for the perforation of plates.

5th. Since it has been shown that the plates lose so little by separation, it is evident that, by almost any cheap and durable filling between them, a considerable addition may be made to their resisting power.

Plates Separated by Bars of Lead.

A few experiments were made with plates of wrought iron separated by bars of soft lead, the object being to absorb a portion of the work of the shot in compressing the lead while the front plate was being perforated.

The result was, that the front plate was bent less than the rear one, and that the lead bars were not compressed at all, excepting immediately around the point of impact. (Rounds 386 and 387, Plate XII, and 403 and 404, back of same plate.)

Conclusions.—This mode of plating possesses no advantages to compensate for the additional expense and difficulty of construction; and a comparison of it with two plates of the same thickness in contact, (Rounds 407 and 408, Plate XI,) was highly favorable to the latter.

Experiments with this form of target were suggested by Generals Wright and Reese, U. S. Engineers.

BEAM, OR GIRDER, TARGET.

This target was made of wrought-iron bars, of an "H" section, 1½-inches deep and ½-inch on the face, placed side by side, and bolted to a wooden backing, as shown by Figs. 1, 2, and 3, Plate XIII.

The spaces between the bars were filled with bits of iron, and it was intended to fill the interstices with an alloy of lead and antimony; but as the workman failed to carry out directions in regard to heating the target before pouring the metal, the latter was chilled before it had filled the whole space.

The result was that the middle portion of the target received no filling but the fragments of iron.

On a large scale, this filling could be replaced by very hard stone and cement.

The bars were cut from a ½-inch plate without heating, and the dimensions were arranged so that the weight of iron in the bars and plates was just equal to that of a ¾-inch solid plate of the same area.

The bars were secured to the backing by ¼-inch screws, made for musket locks by the Ordnance Department.

Conclusions.—1st. The result of firing at this target shows that so far as perforation is concerned, ¾-inch of iron in this form is better than ⅞-inch in a solid plate.

2nd. That the advantages of this kind of structure are more decided in case of cylindrical, than with pointed shot, the latter wedging their way *between* the bars.

3rd. On a large scale, the cost per ton of metal in the form of these beams would be considerably less than for solid plates of equal resisting power.

4th. There would be a difficulty in making an embrasure of this form of material without considerable extra metal by way of reinforce.

5th. Another objection would be the danger from bursting shells.

6th. As the penetration is much greater than it would be in a plate of equivalent resisting power, the effect of concussion would doubtless be correspondingly less.

7th. The wooden backing would be liable to decay, but could be replaced by a backing of vertical beams similar to those of which the front is made.

TUBULAR TARGET.

A small target, (Rounds 394, 395, and 396, Plate XII.) 9 by 16 inches square, was constructed of gas pipe one inch in exterior diameter, placed side by side, and having a very thin plate in front and a ⅝-inch plate in rear, the whole being held together by screws and rivets, as shown in the plate.

The weight of metal in this target was equal to that of a solid ⅞-inch plate, as in case of the beam target just described; but it was not provided with a wooden backing.

It was expected that a shot striking the thin front plate would expend considerable work in driving this plate back and flattening the pipes against the rear and thicker plate; but this result was not realized.

In the three rounds fired at this target, the front plate was perforated without appreciable bending, and the gas pipes were cut through and flattened sideways instead of being driven back against the rear plate. The shot were all stopped, however, which was better than the same metal in a solid plate would have done; though the rear plate was torn off from the pipes by the last shot, the rivets having been weakened by the previous ones. It is probable that with a good backing this target would have given very satisfactory results; though it is doubtful whether the advantage gained by this form of structure would compensate for the great cost of wrought iron pipes of a diameter suitable for larger shields.

The conclusions drawn in the case of the beam target are generally applicable to this one.

It would probably be an advantage to fill the pipes and the spaces between them with concrete or some other suitable material.

PERFORATED, OR CELLULAR PLATES.

In order to get a maximum strength of plate and length of path for the projectile to travel, and thus absorb the shock gradually, several plates of iron and of Bessemer steel, from 1¼ to 1½ inches in thickness, were perforated with holes from ½ to ⅝-inch in diameter, or about half the diameter of the shot; some being entirely through and others having a thin skin of plate at the rear for greater strength. (Rounds 433 to 437, Plate XI.) The holes were *drilled* in these plates, but on a larger scale this would be too expensive; and unless Bessemer steel, or some similar material, can be *cast* in the required form, this kind of plating will doubtless be impracticable.

Conclusions.—The results, in connection with former experiments upon Bessemer steel, were highly favorable, and would, in my opinion, justify experiments on a larger scale with Bessemer steel blocks cast in the cellular form. As before stated, the whole value of this kind of plating depends upon whether the metal can be cast in the requisite form without rolling, hammering, boring, or planing, and it is therefore of the first importance to ascertain positively whether this can be done on a larger scale before going further into the details of this form of structure.

The points in favor of the cellular form of plating are:

1st. Great transverse strength with small amount of material.

2nd. The shot is stopped gradually, considerable space being allowed for that purpose.

3rd. The effects of the shot were extremely limited, the cracks hardly extending beyond the circle of holes immediately around the point of impact.

4th. The effect of bursting shells would probably be less disastrous than with almost any other kind of plating; since the walls of the holes would confine the explosion laterally and cause it to blow out in front where the fragments would do no damage.

5th. The embrasure could be made sufficiently strong by leaving a ring of solid metal of suitable thickness around it.

6th. The cost, provided it can be made as suggested, would be much less than that of wrought iron made in any of the usual forms.

7th. The appearance of this kind of plating could be made presentable by filling the holes, or at least covering them, with asphalt or any other cheap and durable material, and the same means properly applied would probably add to the efficiency of the structure.

PUDDLED IRON.

Two specimens of puddled iron were forwarded by General Foster, U. S. Engineers. The first was compressed only in the furnace, and weighed

35 pounds: the second was partially compressed with a steam hammer, and weighed 47 pounds. Each block was three inches thick, and six by twelve inches square. (Plate XII, Rounds 414, 415, 416, 417, 420, and 421.)

Conclusions.—The result shows that the specimen not hammered was deficient in tensile strength, as it showed a disposition to crack, and at the last round broke in two. This was probably owing to the fact that the particles of metal require some little compression after puddling to cause them to cohere. The second specimen gave better results, and may be considered as about equivalent, in regard to perforation, to one-third of its thickness, or one inch of good wrought-iron plate. The cost must therefore be as one to three in comparison with good iron, in order to compete with it in regard to penetrating resistance alone. It is claimed, however, that this form of metal can be furnished in large masses by the Radcliffe process; and, if so, this will be an argument in its favor.

It will be noticed that the penetration was considerably greater than in solid wrought iron, which would also be an advantage, other circumstances being equal, in diminishing the effects of concussion. The additional thickness and weight would give stability to the structure.

Analogous to the foregoing was a single experiment with a fragment of an Ellershausen ingot. This fragment was too small for anything but a rough experiment, which was made by casting it in a matrix of lead, and firing a single shot at it. The result showed that metal in this state possesses very little tenacity, and would be dear at almost any price for purposes of armor-plating.

The reason for this is apparent from the nature of the process by which these ingots are formed; though the result is not an objection to this process, which, when fully carried out is said to produce an excellent quality of iron.

ANNEALED IRON.

It is well known that iron plates on leaving the rolls are generally somewhat hardened by the process, and warped so as to require straightening when cold. It is quite likely, then, that the fibers of the metal are not in the best condition to resist impact. In order to test this point, several plates which were found to be about thick enough to stop a spherical shot projected by a 300-

grain charge, were annealed by placing them in a charcoal fire, which brought them to a red heat; after which they were covered up and allowed to remain in the coal until the fire went out, and the plates were gradually cooled off. In every case the shot was stopped by these plates; whereas in every case but one it had gone through before the plates were annealed. There is good reason to believe that heavy plates would be greatly improved by annealing, though rolling mills are not generally provided with furnaces for that purpose.

The effect of this process is probably to release the elementary laminæ of the plate from undue and unequal strains, caused by the unequal heating of the different portions of the plate, and allowing them to take up more favorable positions for assisting each other.

CHILLED IRON.

The results of a few experiments with chill-cast iron, suggested by General Wright, U. S. Engineers, are shown on Plate XIV; from which it will be seen that even when of great thickness, and protected by wrought-iron plates almost thick enough of themselves to stop the shot, the cast iron is broken into fragments. The presumption is, therefore, strongly against the utility of this metal, though it is by no means certain that on a larger scale it may not give better results. The effect of chilling or casting in iron molds is such that little reliance can be placed on any experiments upon this material, unless made with castings essentially the same in form, dimensions, and quality of metal as those to be used in practice.

For example, in testing car wheels it is necessary to try one or more of the wheels themselves, instead of testing small models or specimens of the same metal. This arises from the fact that the chill process is chiefly superficial in its effect, and is affected by many circumstances not easily regulated or even understood, and still less easily combined in the proper manner to produce the best results. The details of the process are often varied, and many *secrets* as well as *patents* are connected therewith.

Considering the process, as its name implies, to consist in the sudden cooling of the metal by casting it in molds of iron, a good conductor of heat, it would seem to be a step in the wrong direction so far as armor-plating is concerned; because, while making the metal harder at the surface, it makes

10

it more brittle and increases the initial strains due to shrinkage in cooling. This was the manner in which the plates tested in these experiments were made, and it is the only one which could strictly be called "chilling;" but it is understood that much of the chilled iron of the present day, including the shot of Palliser and of Grüson, and probably the casemate of the latter, is produced by neutralizing, and perhaps partially reversing the chill process, by heating the molds before pouring in the iron or otherwise—or it is annealing, rather than chilling; although the iron molds, however much they are heated, must have great effect in determining the nature of the crystallization of the surface of the casting.

Although the Grüson casemate, twenty inches thick, has withstood the effect of pointed projectiles of moderate caliber, at considerable range, and striking at acute angles, there appears to be no good reason to expect any decided advantage from this material as compared with wrought iron.

LEAD CONCRETE.

Several targets in which lead concrete was combined with iron plates were tested with a view of ascertaining the practical value of concrete, and the best mode of uniting it with iron, as well as the proper thickness and number of plates of iron to be used.

The first target constructed was composed of a ½-inch plate of wrought iron, a ¼-inch plate of Bessemer steel, and three inches of lead concrete. The concrete in this, as in the three following targets, was made by filling a sheet-iron case, of which the plates formed the bottom, with fragments of wrought-iron turnings, about an inch long, and of various sizes, and, after heating the mass nearly to a red heat, pouring in the melted lead. The face of the target was one foot square, and its weight 313 pounds. (Plate XVII.)

The connection between the plates and concrete was formed by screwing five ⅜-inch bolts, two and a half inches long, into the plates, leaving the heads projecting into the concrete, where they were cemented by the lead.

It was found that the ¾ inch of iron and steel was almost as much, by itself, as the shot would go through; and, in order to get at the effect upon the concrete, the ½-inch front plate was removed. (See Plate XVIII, Rounds 327, 328, and 329.)

Three other targets of similar construction were made and tested, each of which contained a thickness of 1½ inches of lead concrete, and a total thickness of ½ inch of wrought iron.

In the first of these the iron was in a single plate, ½ inch thick, backed by 1½ inches of lead concrete. The plate was secured to the concrete by five bolts similar to those just described. The entire weight of this target was 100 pounds. (Plate XVII, Rounds 330 to 333.)

In the second, two ¼-inch plates were bolted together, with the 1½ inches of lead concrete between them. The weight was 97 pounds. (Plate XVII, Rounds 336 and 338.)

In the third, four ⅛-inch plates were bolted together with three layers of lead concrete, ½ inch thick each, between them. Weight 108 pounds. (Plate XVII, Rounds 337 and 339.)

Experiments with this material were suggested by Colonel Casey, U. S. Engineers.

Conclusions.—1st. That lead concrete, in combination with iron plates, is particularly secure against damage from concussion, the effect of shot being confined almost entirely to penetration. This results from the great weight, the ease with which a shot penetrates this material, the high degree of ductility, and the low elasticity.

Of course, bolts and other fastenings are comparatively safe from jars and strains.

2nd. The best combination is a single thick plate with the concrete in *front* to allow as much penetration as possible.

The shot hole in this case being conical, and smaller at the bottom, it would probably be as good a disposition as could be made to avert the damage of exploding shells. (See rounds 302 and 332, Plate XVII, back.)

It has been found at Shoeburyness that shells exploded in ordinary concrete, blow out in front of the target without doing much damage.

The lead concrete would doubtless give still better results.

When the shot penetrates the plate first, the hole is no larger than the shot, and an explosion would be more likely to tear the plate from the backing.

3rd. The cost of lead concrete has not been definitely ascertained, as it would depend upon the kind of scrap-iron used for filling and upon the mode of combining it with the plates. At the present prices of materials it would not probably fall short of $30 or $40 per cubic foot.

4th. There would be some difficulty in making an embrasure of this material, and it would probably require a strong ring of solid wrought iron around it to give the necessary strength without obstructing space required for the muzzle of the gun.

In connection with lead concrete should be mentioned a block of lead and wire netting, prepared by Mr. Ralph Crooker, of the Bay State Iron Works, Boston, Massachusetts, and forwarded by General Foster, U. S. Engineers.

This block was 3 inches thick, 6 by 12 inches square, and consisted of thirty layers of wire netting, which, after being tinned in order to cause the lead to adhere to it, was placed in a mold and filled with lead, the whole weighing 81 pounds.

The result of firing at this target was not essentially different from that of the lead concrete, and the same remarks apply to it as to that material.

Mr. Crooker proposes to construct armor of lead, or an alloy of lead and other metal to increase hardness, and tinned iron wire, either woven or laid together at right angles or diagonally, and heating to the fusing point with heated air.

SAND BETWEEN IRON PLATES.

Various combinations of sand and iron plates have been suggested for defensive works, and some of them have been tested experimentally. One of the latter was proposed by Colonel Mendell, U. S. Engineers

From the results of these experiments, as well as from the results of firing into loose sand, the following conclusions are drawn:

1st. That the sand should be covered with a very thin plate in front and should have a thick plate in rear.

This is manifest from the fact that sand offers much greater resistance to projectiles moving with high velocities, and is easily penetrated after the velocity has been reduced; whereas with iron the reverse of this obtains.

2nd. The sand must be confined in small compartments in order to prevent the case from being emptied by a single shot and thus exposed to perforation by a subsequent one.

3rd. Perhaps very poor mortar or asphalt, in layers between the plates, would prevent the sand from running out. Hexagonal prisms of thin iron filled with sand, and having their ends closed, might be placed between the thick and thin plates, like the cells of a honey-comb.

4th. As considerable thickness of sand would be required, and for other reasons, it would be somewhat difficult to form an embrasure in a scarp of this description.

5th. The work is expended in pulverizing the sand and in imparting a high velocity to those grains first acted upon. The effect is, therefore, local and highly favorable to bolts and other fastenings.

6th. The effect of bursting shells in such a structure must be disastrous.

7th. Sand would have no rival in regard to cost.

PENETRATION IN SAND.

The following are mean results taken from a number of experiments on the penetration of *spherical shot* in loose sand. The sand was clean, dry, and fine-grained, and was not rammed but allowed to take its own density as it was poured into the sheet-iron box described, among the other apparatus, on page 14.

TABLE V.

Number of rounds from which mean is taken.	Kind of shot.	Weight of charge.	Penetration.
10	Spherical . . .	400 grains . . .	22 inches.
13	Spherical . . .	300 grains . . .	20¾ inches.
8	Spherical . . .	200 grains . . .	18¾ inches.
8	Spherical . . .	100 grains . . .	15 inches.
7	Spherical . . .	50 grains . . .	12 3-16 + inches.
4	Spherical . . .	25 grains . . .	10 + inches.
2	Spherical . . .	12½ grains . . .	8¾ inches.
2	Spherical . . .	6¼ grains . . .	7 1-5 inches.
3	Spherical . . .	3 grains . . .	Shot moved about half the length of the gun

These experiments agree with what was already known, that sand possesses in a remarkable degree the requirements for stopping projectiles. The great advantages of high velocity and elongated projectiles, which are so efficient in penetrating iron or stone, become almost useless against sand.

It will be noticed by an inspection of the foregoing results that the increase of penetration is very much slower than the increase of velocity, and that there is probably a point in the penetration, not far beyond the greatest already obtained, which cannot be passed, even with an indefinite increase of velocity.

The diagram, (Fig. 4, Plate XIII,) as well as the table just given, shows that six and one-fourth grains of powder will cause the shot to penetrate over seven inches; while 400 grains, or 64 times as much, causes the same shot to penetrate only 22 inches, or about three times as far.

A few rounds with elongated shot, which, it will be recollected, gave considerably better results than spherical ones in penetrating iron, showed that the same charge of powder gave considerably less penetration in sand than was obtained with spherical ones; this last being due to the tendency of elongated shot to deviate from their course, and turn end for end during the penetration. A very high velocity of rotation would doubtless improve this defect, though probably not to any great extent.

In order to compare these results with those of large experiments, we have the following data from the reports of experimental firing at Fort Monroe.

For the 15-inch solid shot, weighing about 434 pounds, throwing out those rounds which differed most from the mean results:

40 pounds charge, mean of four rounds, 13 feet 4 inches penetration.
45 pounds charge, mean of six rounds, 16 feet 4 inches penetration.
50 pounds charge, mean of six rounds, 17 feet 2 inches penetration.
100 pounds charge, mean of seven rounds, 15 feet 9.6 inches penetration.

The shot in the last case weighed 450 pounds, and as the penetration was actually less than it was with 45 pounds charge, there must have been a difference in the density of the targets.

Taking the penetration of the 1-inch gun at 18¾ inches for a velocity of 1,050 feet, the 15-inch gun ought, under the same circumstances, to penetrate about 23 feet.

The actual penetration of the 15-inch gun, with 50 pounds charge, which gives about that velocity, would have been, according to the table, allowing for difference in density of projectiles, 19 feet 4 inches. The difference, or 3 feet 8 inches, would be fully made up by the fact that the sand was light, clean, fine-grained, and perfectly dry in the first case, while in the latter it was thoroughly rammed, and probably contained more or less moisture. This shows that the power of penetration in sand for spherical shot varies nearly with the diameter of the projectile, as might have been expected.

One point noticed in these experiments, and which probably obtains also in the larger ones, was the formation of a conical lump of powdered sand upon the side of the shot which first struck the sand. The size of this lump probably increases with the striking velocity, and since it rarely remains in front of the shot, owing to the rotation of the latter, it must exercise considerable retarding influence even when, as is generally the case, it is scraped off during the penetration. It was thought that a large share of the discrepancies observed in these experiments was due to the irregular action of this lump of sand, and if it existed in the large experiments it may have produced like effects.

It was also noticed that when successive shots were fired into the sand without stirring, or replacing it, the penetration rapidly diminished, owing no doubt to the fact that the sand was compacted by each shot.

The results of a few rounds of cylindro-spherical shot indicate, as before stated, that although they have considerable more stored-up work for a given charge, and at a lower velocity, they will not penetrate as far as the spherical ones, owing to the almost certain tendency to tumble in passing through the sand. Of course, it is barely possible that one of these shots may go straight, and, should it happen to do so, the penetration would be greater; but a glance at the circumstances of the case is sufficient to show that such a contingency is highly improbable.

Referring again to the experiments at Fort Monroe, we find the following mean results for the 12-inch rifle:

Mean of 20 rounds, charge of 50 pounds, solid shot 465 pounds, 13 feet 1.4 inches penetration.

Mean of 9 rounds, charge of 55 pounds, hollow shot 511 pounds, 16 feet 10 inches penetration.

Mean of 4 rounds, charge of 70 pounds, shell 487 pounds, 16 feet 9 inches penetration.

Mean of 4 rounds, charge of 70 pounds, solid shot 628 pounds, 17 feet 6 inches penetration.

These results seem to indicate, as before remarked, that neither high velocities nor elongated projectiles can overcome the resistance of sand beyond a limited thickness. It has been found, at Fort Monroe and elsewhere, that wetting sand, or mixing clay with it, greatly diminishes its resistance to penetration.

Sand is not, however, as perfect a material for defensive works as is generally supposed. It is very easy to build a heap of almost any material, where there is plenty of room, to withstand the effect of shot; but a properly constructed work cannot depend upon a passive resistance alone, and must therefore have provisions for *guns* and cover for the men to work them. This point appears too commonplace for even a notice, and yet it is no more common than the proposition to construct a *scarp* without the slightest attention being paid to the all-important question of how to construct an *embrasure.*

Take for example a parapet for barbette guns, and remove all those portions through which a 15-inch shot will pass with impunity, and which would therefore be next to useless so far as sheltering the cannoniers is concerned, recollecting that such a shot will penetrate at least fifteen feet of sand, and see how much such a parapet would be better than none at all. The difficulty here alluded to would be greatly increased if, instead of a simple parapet, it was proposed to construct an embrasure, either open or covered; since, in addition to sufficient thickness, the sand would have to be sustained by revetments.

STEEL.

The progress made within the past few years in the manufacture of steel as well as iron, has been such as to indicate that in a very short time steel may be produced as cheaply, if not cheaper, than wrought iron is at the present day. In fact, steel is already taking the place of iron for rails, steamboat shafts, and various other industrial purposes, to a very great extent; and inventions of new processes and apparatus for its manufacture, and improvements in those already in use, have become so common as to attract but little attention.

The effect of all this must be a great reduction in the labor and expense of manufacturing steel, which for many years has been conducted on the old and very expensive plan. As steel is, chemically speaking, between cast and wrought iron, it must eventually take that position in regard to cost; and whatever tends to reduce the cost of steel must also produce a like effect on iron.

Since these improvements have a manifest bearing upon the subject of armor plating, a brief outline of some of them will be here given. It will be noticed that some are for the production of steel alone, some for iron, and some for both.

1st. *Common process.*—Two or more kinds of ore are generally combined, and when roasted are mixed with carbonate of lime and subjected to an intense heat in a blast furnace.

Ordinary cast or pig-iron, containing four or five per cent of carbon, is the product.

In order to get rid of a portion of the carbon, the metal is remelted and chilled, after which small quantities are put through the process of puddling in a reverberatory furnace, and after the carbon has been nearly all burned out, it is formed into balls and passed through a "squeezer," or hammered, to expel cinder and condense the mass. It is then rolled or hammered into any desired shape, large masses being formed by welding together a sufficient number of small ones. This is ordinary wrought iron, and contains only a trace of carbon. To improve the quality of this, small pieces are piled together, welded, and drawn out again, the operation being repeated as often as desired.

Having passed the requirements of steel in the process of decarbonization, a portion of carbon must be reintroduced.

This is done by heating the bars of wrought iron in tanks or retorts, with charcoal, until the requisite amount of carbon is taken up. The operation consumes several days, and blistered steel is thus arrived at.

In order to get a homogeneous mass, especially if a large mass is required, these bars are broken up, assorted, and remelted in small crucibles, the quantity being made up by *numbers*, rather than *size*, of crucibles. It is then cast, and rolled or hammered, into the desired shape.

The expense of this, especially the remelting, which requires large numbers of crucibles, costing several dollars apiece, and which stand but a few meltings, is necessarily very great.

The labor is all severe, and great skill is required in almost every stage of the process, which may be summed up as consisting of roasting, smelting, refining, puddling, shingling, piling, or blooming, rolling, baking, or blistering, casting, and hammering.

2nd. *Bessemer process.*—Cast iron, free as possible from sulphur and phosphorus, but containing a certain percentage of manganese, is melted or may be drawn directly from the blast furnace, and run into a "converter," a large egg-shaped crucible of boiler iron, lined with fire-bricks, and a stream of air is forced in, at a high pressure, through a number of small holes in the bottom, like the nozzle of a watering pot.

The oxygen of the air combines with the carbon of the iron, forming an intense flame of carbonic oxide. In about twenty minutes, depending upon the volume of air admitted and the quantity of metal under treatment, as well as upon the percentage of carbon to be got rid of, the excess of carbon is burned out, and the contents of the converter, or several of them, may be cast into a steel ingot of any desired dimensions.

One difficulty which has been met with in this process, has been to determine the exact time to stop the decarbonization in order to leave only the required amount; but this has been practically overcome by allowing the carbon to be entirely burned out, and then adding such a quantity of melted iron as will contain an amount of carbon sufficient for the whole mass.

It is stated that the spectrum analysis is also being applied, with a fair prospect of success, for the purpose of ascertaining when the exact percentage of carbon is present.

The ingots of Bessemer steel are sometimes quite porous, but are improving in this respect; and even when the pores, or blow-holes, are quite large, the ingot may be brought to a welding heat and rolled or hammered into a solid mass.

They may also be broken up and remelted, forming "crucible" steel.

3rd. *Richardson's process.*—This is essentially conducting the Bessemer process in an ordinary puddling furnace, and is accomplished by using hollow stirring irons or rabbles, through which a stream of air is forced while the operation of puddling is going on.

The operation may be continued until wrought iron is formed or stopped at the right point for steel, and is said to effect a great saving of time and labor over the ordinary mode of puddling, the carbon being burned out much more rapidly.

4th. *Martin's process.*—A quantity of cast iron is melted in a reverberatory furnace, and at the proper time a definite proportion of red-hot scrap wrought iron is added. The excess of carbon in the cast iron is taken up by the wrought, and, by a proper amount of stirring, the mass becomes homogeneous and may be cast into ingots as in the Bessemer process. It has given very favorable results, though it has not been very extensively used.

5th. *Uchatiu's process* consists in bringing oxides of iron in contact with melted cast iron.* The pig iron is melted and poured into a cold-water tank, striking a horizontal wheel revolving at considerable speed. The iron is thus broken into small granules and falls to the bottom. These granules are then mixed with pulverized oxide of iron and some alkaline earths and remelted.

6th. *Shower process.*—This is believed to be similar to the last process.

7th. *Nitrate process* consists in bringing a quantity of nitrate of soda or of potash in contact with melted pig iron, the oxygen being taken from the nitre by the carbon in a manner similar to the other processes. Other substances, containing a large proportion of oxygen, have been used instead of those mentioned, and it is supposed by some that the presence of nitrogen is useful, if not essential, in producing a superior quality of steel.

8th. *Siemens's process.*—By a very ingenious kind of furnace, in which *gas* from almost any kind of cheap fuel, mixed with air, is substituted for *coal*, Mr. Siemens generates heat of such intensity as to reduce oxide of iron without introducing more carbon than is required for steel, thus avoiding the production of cast iron altogether, and getting steel directly from the ore.

This is going a step further back than the Bessemer process, and if successful, will doubtless give a cheaper article of steel.

9th. *McHaffie & Company*, of Glasgow, produce a kind of steel by placing cast-iron boxes, supposed to contain moistened oxide of manganese, and perhaps other substances, in a cupola for melting cast iron. These boxes sink down with the mass, being prevented from melting at first by the evaporation of the moisture contained in them, until they come in contact with the liquid metal, when they melt and their contents are united with the iron.

The metal is then cast in molds, and, after annealing, is found to be exceedingly hard and close-grained, and warranted to sustain twenty-five tons per square inch. Some doubt exists in regard to this process, as the proprietors decline to communicate in regard to it.

10th. *Chenot's process.*—Pure magnetic ore, found in a state of powder in a certain district among the Pyrenees, is put in a furnace, and, being protected from the fuel by a tube, the powder is reduced to a spongy state of nearly pure iron, though it is not melted. It is then compressed by hydrostatic pressure into a solid mass, after which it is covered with oils and other carbonaceous substances, and melted in close crucibles.

11th. *Smith's process.*—Mr. J. P. Smith, of Glasgow, claims that by adding certain chemicals to the pig iron, after melting in an air furnace, the carbon, in the form of graphite, may be separated from the metal and thrown to the surface, where it may be skimmed off. A further addition of chemicals throws the silicon off in the same manner.

This steel is very hard and is cast with facility, but it is more suitable for tools than for armor-plating.

12th. *Heaton's process*—Melted pig iron is poured into a converter containing nitrate of soda and sand, covered by a perforated plate. It is afterward placed under a tilt hammer. The operation requires about five minutes' time for each charge. Quite a controversy has sprung up in regard to the novelty and usefulness of this process, in the leading scientific journals.

13th. *Gjers' process.*—Wrought-iron scrap is coated with coal tar, 100 parts; iron ore, 50 parts; ore of manganese 25 parts; slaked lime, 25 parts, with more or less oxides or lime, according as hard or soft steel is required These ingredients are melted in a modified form of Siemens' furnace.

14th. *Radcliff's process* is simply a process for welding up the entire mass of iron required, directly from the puddled balls. To effect this, he has a large number of furnaces arranged in a semicircle around the hammer as a center, this arrangement being for convenience in bringing the balls together. The number of balls required to build up the required mass are brought to the proper working condition at the same time, and are taken from their respective furnaces simultaneously and thrown together under the hammer. Ordinarily, it will be recollected, each ball is hammered by itself and then a number of them reheated and welded into a mass. This process, like many others, is variously considered according to the interests and peculiar views entertained by different parties—some alleging that it is no process at all, or that it possesses no novelty, and others taking the opposite view.

15th. *Ellershausen's process* consists in certain mechanical means for bringing oxide of iron, in shape of powdered ore, in contact with a stream of molten cast iron. The decarbonization of cast iron, by means of oxide of iron, is one of the oldest forms of steel making; but this process, it is said, overcomes the mechanical difficulties.

The streams of molten iron and powdered ore are allowed to run into the same mold in regulated quantities, the result being a kind of porous ingot, which, after remelting and a slight amount of puddling, is wrought into bars of excellent iron.

16th. *Berard's process* consists in the use of a Siemens' furnace, with two hearths, in which charges of cast iron are placed and treated with oxidizing and reducing flames in succession. Gases containing hydrogen, as carburetted hydrogen, steam, and free hydrogen, are forced into the metal through hollow rabbles, and are said to be highly beneficial in driving off sulphur and other impurities.

Other processes might be enumerated, and by reference to the records in the Patent Office, the number could be extended almost indefinitely. Such an enumeration, as well as the discussion of the relative advantages of the different processes, belongs, however, to the province of metallurgy, and those here given are only such as occurred incidentally without special study of their merits, or search for others to complete the list.

Steel Compared with Iron.

The question may suggest itself: Why has steel been thus far rejected for armor-plating? The reasons generally assigned have been its cost and the tendency which it manifests to fly, or at least to crack in pieces, when struck by projectiles. These conclusions are believed to have been drawn from experiments of a similar nature to those mentioned in connection with laminated armor. They were made with plates barely thick enough to stop the shot, and in some cases not thick enough for that purpose: the object being to avoid weight as far as possible.

It is, therefore, an open question whether steel plates are economical, where sufficient thickness is given to stop the shot, and allow a sufficient margin of safety.

For example, a 4½-inch or even a 6-inch plate of steel may be inferior to wrought iron, for stopping a 7-inch rifle shot; for the reason that such a shot might go through and split, bend, or tear the plates. But it does not follow that a 9 or 10-inch plate would prove less efficient than a wrought-iron plate of equal or perhaps greater thickness, in stopping the same projectile.

In order to get some data on this subject, four kinds of Bessemer steel have been procured and tested in these experiments; three kinds being simply cast in ingots and cut into thin plates in a lathe, and the fourth being rolled into plates in the usual manner.

The ingots were cylindrical in form, one foot in diameter and two feet long, and contained different proportions of carbon. One was intended to contain a mere trace, another about ½ of one per cent., and the third one per cent., all being what would be classed as "low," or soft steel. It is proposed to subject them to chemical analysis, and ascertain the exact amount of carbon in each.

As it was supposed that this metal would prove considerably weaker than wrought iron, the expected advantage of it being in point of cost, and the fact that it could be procured in larger masses, the plates were made thicker than the iron ones, and were, when finished, ½ inch, 1 inch, and 1½ inches thick.

The ingots, especially those containing the least amount of carbon, were quite porous, some of the plates cut from them resembling the section of a watermelon; notwithstanding this, however, the comparison of these plates, with wrought-iron ones of equal thickness, was decidedly favorable.

Of seven shots, fired at half-inch plates from each of these ingots, only one got through; while with common wrought iron the same shot would have gone through in a majority of cases. Plates XV. and XVI.

The plates showed a greater disposition to crack, but by allowing a coefficient of safety as before mentioned, this may readily be obviated.

For example, the same shot against a 1-inch plate was stopped without the slightest crack, or other indication of damage to the plate, excepting the small indent ⅜ inch deep, produced by the shot itself; and, although it has not yet been tried, there is little doubt but that such a plate would stop any reasonable number of the same shot, fired with the same velocity.

The metal thus prepared, that is, simply cast in the shape in which it is wanted, without rolling or hammering, can be procured much cheaper than wrought iron, especially if large masses are desired. Ingots, weighing 40 or 50 tons, have been made and can be produced as readily as smaller ones, provided, of course, a sufficient number of converters are at hand.

It becomes a question, therefore, whether it would not be better to dispense with rolling, hammering, trimming and drilling, which are very expensive, and invest their cost in additional weight of metal. If wrought-iron plates, prepared in the usual manner, for shields cost fifteen cents per pound, and Bessemer steel can be cast in any desired form and bulk for six cents, it would require that six inches of the former should be as good as fifteen inches of the latter, in order to make the iron as economical as the steel. But since the work of perforation increases with something like the square of the thickness, a single inch of wrought iron must be $\frac{225}{36} = 6\frac{1}{4}$ times as good as an inch of the steel, in order to compete with it successfully.

These last figures are merely used to give a general idea of the difference between the two metals, without attempting any great accuracy, and it should also be mentioned that the results of these and other experiments indicate that the work of penetrating masses of steel does not increase as rapidly as that of wrought iron for equal increments of thickness.

This last requires further investigation; though it is safe to assume that in all probability the steel will prove far more economical than iron for permanent defenses.

One great advantage in favor of the steel would be the entire freedom from bolts, and all kinds of togglery which tend to weaken and destroy the efficiency of armor-plating as now constructed.

It is quite probable that two or three grades of steel might be cast in the same plate, so as to have one side hard and of great tensile strength, while the other would be soft, porous, and ductile.

The steel for a large plate would have to be prepared in several independent converters, and could be made of any desired consistency, and it would only be necessary to pour these different grades into the mold, in the order of their densities, taking care to have the "gates" so arranged that the metal poured last would enter the mold horizontally, and flow over the surface of that which had preceded it without disturbing the latter.

Should the pieces be cast hollow, the spaces might be filled, after the metal had cooled, with concrete or other hard substance to form a solid mass.

But few trials of the rolled Bessemer steel have been made; but the indication thus far is that this metal is fully equal to the best wrought iron, or at least to the best tried in these experiments; and it is stated that heavy plates of this metal, say 6 by 12 feet, and 12 to 15 inches thick, can be made with suitable machinery somewhat cheaper than the iron.

There is not at present any such machinery in operation in this country, though it could be erected at a moderate cost.

The ingots, up to ten tons weight, can now be cast in this country.

BOLTS.

In addition to being very expensive, bolts are elements of weakness in two ways:

1st. They are liable to be broken themselves, and the pieces become dangerous missiles, a fact fully demonstrated by nearly all experiments on a large scale; and

2nd. They require holes which weaken the plates and other parts of the structure through which they pass. In almost every case where a plate is struck near a bolt hole, the fracture passes through, if it does not commence at, the hole.

In short, the most favorable view to be taken of bolts is that they are necessary evils, and where they are not absolutely necessary of course they should be avoided.

During the progress of these experiments, some facts relative to the strains upon bolts were developed:

The corners of the plates were held in position against the target frame by four ¾-inch bolts, a portion of the bolt heads pressing against the corners of the plate, the middle of the plate and the edges, excepting the extreme corners, being unsupported either in front or rear. The plates were one foot square, and of various thicknesses up to ¾-inch. The shot struck the plates within about two inches of the center, sometimes going through and sometimes not, according to circumstances. In very many cases the bolt heads were knocked off by the concussion, and the bolts were often considerably bent. This sometimes took place when the plate was only half an inch thick, or two-thirds the diameter of the bolts. The strain coming upon one side of the bolt head of course took the bolts at a disadvantage; but considering the fact that they were from one to one and a half times the thickness of the plates, it would appear that the strain upon them must be very considerable. A case analogous to this would be a 6-inch plate *twelve feet* square, held in position by four bolts *nine inches* in diameter.

This view is corroborated by the results of nearly all the experiments which have been made on a large scale with iron targets. The trial of the Gibraltar and Malta shields, and others of a more recent date, developed the fact that the bolts were the weakest part of the structures, although special attention had been given to their preparation.

STRAINS UPON BOLTS.

There appear to be three kinds of strains by which bolts are broken:

1st. *By direct impact* of the shot transmitted through the plate or bolt, by the elasticity of the metal, to the nut and washer, which, with a piece of the bolt, become projectiles and are thrown to the rear of the target. (Fig. 8, Plate XXV.)

2nd. *The shearing strain*, which comes from the sliding of one plate upon another, or upon the beams or other supports. This sliding is generally due to the bending of the plates (Fig. 7, Plate XXV.) It is clear that if the bolts fit tightly, and the plates are bent in this manner, there must be a tendency to shear one or more bolts, according to the size of the plates, number of bolts, and position of the point of impact.

3rd. In the *third case* the strain may come from the recoil of that portion of the plate near the point struck, and after the shot has expended its work; or it may take place simultaneously with the blow at points beyond the nearest points of support, or beyond "nodal lines" formed by the inertia of the plate and resistance of the supports. (Fig. 9, Plate XXV.)

The bolt at A would be thrown out when the shot struck, while that at B might be broken when the plate recoiled, as shown by the dotted line.

Two or more of these strains may be brought to bear upon the same bolt, by the same projectile; and one shot may leave a number of bolts in a state of tension or weakness, by bending the plates, so that a subsequent shot may easily complete the rupture.

Different Kinds of Bolts.

To obviate or neutralize the effects of these strains, the following plans have been proposed, the object sought in all these devices being the same, viz: to allow a yielding or extension, and thus increase the length of path traveled over by the resistance of the bolt; or, in other words, to increase the *work* of breaking.

1st. *By the use of washers of soft metal, rubber, or wood.* This plan, by itself, has proved entirely inadequate in numerous experiments, probably from the fact that it does not provide against the shearing strain, nor effectually against direct impact. It is, however, a step in the right direction.

2nd. *By reducing the shank*, or middle portion of the bolt, to a section somewhat smaller than its smallest section at the thread.

It is well known that a bolt of the ordinary form (Fig. 1, Plate XXVI) will always break at the bottom of a thread between the base of the nut and the solid part of the bolt. This is evidently due to the fact that, in addition to being the weakest point, it is the only part of the bolt weak enough to be stretched, and the whole elongation therefore takes place at that point. The work of breaking the bolt thus becomes correspondingly small. By reducing the shank to a smaller section than this weak point, as before mentioned, the amount of stretch will be increased, and with it the work of breaking the bolt.

Captain Palliser was, I believe, the first to apply this principle to bolts for armor plates. Fig. 2, Plate XXVI.

It is an objection to this bolt that it does not fill the hole; but, on the other hand, this has the advantage of rendering it less liable to be sheared. The trial of the Gibraltar and other shields has shown that while this bolt was an improvement, it was not all that could be desired. A similar form of bolt has long been used in railroad bridges and similar structures, though it was probably adopted for the purpose of saving metal rather than from any supposed mechanical advantages.

The Parsons bolt (Fig. 3) accomplishes the same purpose by drilling the metal from the axis, instead of turning it from the outside; and this bolt therefore fills the hole. It was claimed that this bolt contributed to the success of the Millwall shield at Shoeburyness.

The Chalmers bolt (Fig. 4) is the same in principle, and is made of two nearly "half-round" bars, welded at the ends, and leaving a space in the middle which is filled with hard wood.

3rd. A plan has suggested itself during this discussion which appears to combine some of the advantages enumerated, and to obviate some of the disadvantages. It would cost more than either of the foregoing bolts, and involves some skill in making.

Let a number of small bars of steel, a little shorter than the required bolt, be piled together with small strips of iron between the ends, and the whole temporarily wired together as shown. (Fig. 1, Plate XXV.)

The pile may be placed in a furnace and brought to a suitable heat for welding iron and steel, so that under the hammer or between rolls the ends will be welded solid; but the middle, being steel against steel, will be drawn out and compacted, but not welded; and, by a proper course of treatment, may be twisted together and formed into a bolt. (See Fig. 2, same Plate.)

With a suitable application of swaging tools, a bolt of this kind may be hammered out and completed without the use of the lathe, excepting to cut the thread and perhaps shape the head slightly. Such a bolt would be much stronger than either of the preceding, since it would fill the hole completely, and it would admit of bending, compression, elongation, and shearing strain to a very considerable extent, without rupture.

It might be found practicable to treat iron bars in a similar manner, and by heating the ends more than the middle, the welding might be effected as above described. If this can be done it would be considerably cheaper than to use steel; but trial alone can settle the relative merits of these methods.

To make a single bolt by either of these plans would be quite difficult, but a skillful workman would soon devise the means for making large numbers of them at comparatively low rates.

4th. *By using wire rope* for the shank of the bolt. (Fig. 5, Plate XXVI.) This plan seems best adapted to the purpose, though I have not heard of its having been thoroughly tested. The only objection to its use appears to be the difficulty of fastening the ends without making the hole in the plate considerably larger than the rope, to admit a collar containing a thread for the nut. This could be overcome by dispensing with the collar for the head, and inserting the bolt, before the head is formed, in a hole just the size of the bolt, and forming the head in the plate itself, the hole being counter-sunk for the purpose. After the head is formed the nut may be screwed up in the ordinary manner. (Fig. 6, Plate XXVI.)

This bolt will admit of considerable elongation without rupture, and is especially secure against shearing and direct impact.

It may not be generally understood that the head of a wire bolt is formed by unlaying the strands and driving in conical iron wedges, after which the ends of the wire are bent short down over the ends of the wedges and melted lead or solder poured in to unite the whole in one solid mass, and thus prevent the wedges from working out. The hole being made conical, as shown in Figs. 5 and 6, the wire and wedges will draw in together and become tighter and tighter as the strain is increased.

5th. The shearing strain is sometimes obviated by rounding the edges of the plates as shown at *a* and *b*, Fig. 6, Plate XXVI.

6th. The danger of pieces of bolt, with the nut, being thrown off by the transmitted force of the shot, has been overcome by using screw bolts without nuts, the holes in the plates being tapped out and the bolts screwed into them. Of course these bolts, if struck by a shot, would be riveted up instead of being driven through the plate, unless the shot itself went almost through, in which case it would be unreasonable to expect anything to resist it. These bolts must be easily sheared or broken by the concussion

7th. Nuts or washers, with hemispherical bases, fitting in sockets of the same form, have recently been proposed by Major Palliser for securing an equal bearing of the nut upon all sides of the bolt.

Form and size of thread.—The most advantageous form of section for the thread of bolts will depend upon whether the foregoing principles are carried out, so as to prevent the elongation of the bolt between the threads. If such elongation can take place, owing to the shank of the bolt being too strong, a triangular section will not answer, since the whole elongation must take place between the threads, and the fracture would start at that point—in fact, would already be started by the sharp angle of the thread itself In this case it will be better to use a rectangular section, (Fig. 3,) or, still better, a trapezoidal section, as shown in Fig. 4, Plate XXV, which will allow considerable length of bolt, between the threads, for stretching, and present no acute angle for a starting point of rupture.

We will assume that the shank of the bolt has been reduced by one of the foregoing methods, so as to obviate the stretching of the bolt between the threads. It will then be necessary to consider only the case of the thread of triangular section, which is in itself much stronger than any other form. This is evident from an inspection of Fig. 6, Plate XXV, from which it will be seen that the triangular form would require a maximum area of fracture in order to strip the thread. Although it is practically impossible to bring the thread to a sharp angle, it will be sufficiently accurate to consider it so in the first instance, both here and in the following discussion of the nut, and afterward make a suitable allowance for the bluntness of the edge.

It is evident, from an inspection of the triangular thread, that, with a proper angle at the edge, the strength of the whole thread is, theoretically, independent of the number of threads to the inch, and the only reasons for making them coarser for large bolts than for small ones are, the practical difficulty of making fine work fit accurately on large bolts, and the inconvenience of turning the nut so many times to run it on or off.

A thread of triangular section may be compared to a beam fixed at one end and uniformly loaded—the thickness being uniform. The strength of this beam will be given by the following equation:

$C\,b = \frac{W\,l}{d^2}$ where C is a constant, depending upon the quality of the material;

b = the breadth of the beam and corresponds to the developed length of the thread;

d = the depth of the beam, or the thickness of the thread at the base;

l = the length of the beam, or the distance which the thread projects from the surface of the bolt or nut; and

W = the entire weight supported by the beam or thread.

It is well known that this formula gives a beam of equal resistance, or a beam that will be as liable to break at one part as another, under a load uniformly distributed. We may replace l by $c\,d$, since for similar beams the length will bear a constant relation to the depth, which relation is here represented by the new constant c. The equation will then stand $C\,b = \frac{W\,c\,d}{d^2} = \frac{W\,c}{d}$, from which we have $W = \frac{C\,b\,d}{c}$....................(9.)

If, now, b is made to increase as d diminishes, the value of W will not change, which amounts to saying, that if the length of the helix, or thread, varies directly with the number of threads to the inch, which is exactly what takes place, the weight supported, or the strength of the screw, will not be altered. It also appears from equation (9) that the smaller the value of the constant c, the greater will be the value of W, which shows that t should be as small as possible compared with d.

We may, therefore, conclude that the *thread* should be as *fine* and as *shallow* as other considerations will allow; and it will appear from what follows that these principles can be carried much beyond the usual practice without the slightest danger of "stripping" the thread or bursting the nut.

Depth and thickness of nut.—Since the weight of the nut is a source of damage to bolts when the concussion of the shot is transmitted through the plate or bolt, as shown by Fig. 8, Plate XXV, and as it is otherwise desirable, for many purposes, to reduce that weight to the smallest practicable limit, it becomes an interesting question how far this reduction may be carried without weakening the structure.

The question, then, is, required the depth and thickness of a nut that will hold just as much as the bolt to which it belongs.

Take the notation as in Fig. 4, Plate XXIV.

R = radius of bolt at bottom of thread;

t = depth of thread, as before;

T = weight sustained by one square inch of the metal; the same for bolt and nut; and

C = a constant, depending upon the quality of the metal, as before.

From what has preceded, we may, for the purpose of finding the depth of nut required, disregard the number of threads to the inch, and simply find the dimensions of a single thread, or a spire of the helix, and the base of this thread will be the minimum depth of nut which will answer the purpose.

The length of this spire may be taken as the circumference of the bolt without sensible error, and we may write, (equation 9:)

$T \pi R^2 = W = \frac{C b d}{e}$, and since $b = 2 \pi R$

$T \pi R^2 = \frac{C 2 \pi R d}{e}$, solving for d, we have,

$d = \frac{T e}{2 C} R$ ....(10)

from which the value of d may be directly obtained by substituting the known values of the constants, R, C and e.

Assuming $T = 40{,}000$ pounds,

$C = 25{,}000$ pounds, and

$e = \frac{1}{2}$,

we have $d = 0.4\ R$; or, for a 3-inch bolt, since R would be 1.5-inch, the value of d would be only 0.6 of an inch.

The difference between this result and common practice will be apparent from a glance at the nuts on the Gibraltar shield, which were 2½ inches deep, with a jam nut 1½ inches, making in all 4 inches, or nearly seven times the depth required to break the bolt. (See dotted lines, Fig. 4, Plate XXIV.) If we allow one-half for safety, or make the nut 1.2 inches deep, there will still be a margin of three and one-third times.

The practice of using such deep nuts has probably been copied from the practice among machinists, where nuts are frequently taken off and put on, thus wearing out and weakening the thread, and where the continual jar necessitates jam-nuts to prevent unscrewing. If nuts used in armor-plating are properly fitted, so as to turn as hard as may be and yet draw the bolts tightly, it would probably require a very large number of shot, striking it under the most favorable circumstances, to unscrew the nut a single turn.

The *thickness of the nut*, in a direction perpendicular to the axis of the bolt, is also generally made much greater than is required. Retaining the same notation, and referring to Fig. 4, Plate XXIV, required the thickness of nut necessary, first, to resist crushing, and, second, to resist bursting or splitting.

The force tending to crush the base of the nut, or the side in contact with the plate, will be equal to the whole strength of the bolt, or $T \pi R^2$, and representing the semi-diameter of the hexagonal nut by x, we have the effective area of the base of the nut $= \pi x^2 - \pi (R + l)^2$;

Or, $\pi [x^2 - (R + l)^2]$, which, multiplied by the crushing strength of the metal per square inch, must be made equal to the whole strength of the bolt;

Whence, $\pi [x^2 - (R + l)^2] S = \pi R^2 T$;

$$\text{Or, } x = \sqrt{\frac{R^2 T}{S} + (R + l)^2} \qquad \ldots\ldots\ldots\ldots (11)$$

and, as will be seen from the figure,

$x - (R + l) =$ thickness of nut exclusive of thread.

Assuming $T = 40{,}000$ pounds as before,

$S = 45{,}000$ pounds,

$R = 1.5$ inch, and

$l = 0.1$ inch, there will result, $x - (R + l) = 0.54$ inch = thickness of nut.

The assumed value of S is probably *too small*, notwithstanding the fact that according to most tables it is *too large*. It only remains to ascertain whether the section of the nut thus arrived at, viz, 1.2 inch deep and 0.54 inch thick, will resist the wedging tendency of the thread to burst or split it.

The whole strain upon the bolt is under the foregoing supposition $\pi R^2 T$, and this, divided by the circumference of the bolt at the bottom of the thread, which is $2 \pi R$, will give the strain per unit of length of the thread, $\frac{\pi R^2 T}{2 \pi R} = \frac{R\,T}{2}$; and the strain in the same direction upon the space $R\,d\varphi$; in which φ is a variable angle between the space $d\varphi$, and a fixed plane through the axis of the bolt, see Fig. 4, Plate XXIV, will be $\frac{R\,T}{2} \times R\,d\varphi = \frac{R^2 T}{2}\,d\varphi$. Now the tendency of this force, which it will be recollected is acting in a direction parallel to the axis of the bolt, to force the portion of the nut opposite the space $R\,d\varphi$ outward, will be $\frac{R^2 T}{2}\,d\varphi$ multiplied by the tangent of the angle α, which the axis of the bolt makes with a tangent plane to the helical surface of the thread, diminished by twice the limiting angle of friction β; since friction will oppose sliding both between the surfaces of the threads of the bolt and nut, and between the base of the nut and the plate.

We thus have $\frac{R^2 T}{2}\,d\varphi \tan(\alpha - 2\beta)$ and this force is the force tending to crowd the nut outward, and is estimated in the direction of radius. But the rupture will take place in the plane of the axis of the bolt, since this is the weakest section, and we must, therefore, estimate the rupturing force in a direction normal to that plane, which we will assume to coincide with the plane from which φ is estimated.

This is done by simply multiplying the foregoing expression by sin φ and we then have $\frac{R^2 T}{2} \tan (\alpha - 2\beta.) \sin \varphi \, d\varphi$.

Integrating between 0° and 180°, φ being the only variable, there results $\frac{R^2 T}{2} \tan (\alpha - 2\beta)$ ver sin 180°, and since ver sin 180° = 2 R we may write $R^2 T \tan (\alpha - 2\beta)$ which must be made less than the strength of the nut in the plane of rupture.

The section of the nut, as before determined, was 1″.2 × 0″.54 exclusive of the thread, and this must be doubled since the strain comes on both sides of the nut.

We then have 1″.2 × 0″.54 × 2 × T for the strength of the nut; and this must be made equal to or less than the expression just found.

Or 1.″2 × 0″. 54 × 2 × $T = R^2 T. \tan (\alpha - 2\beta)$. . . . .(12);
or $\tan (\alpha - 2\beta) = 0.39$, from which the value of $(\alpha - 2\beta)$ is found to be but 21°½. Since β = say 9°, α may have a value of 39°½ without danger of splitting the nut.

The value which we assumed for c in the preceding discussion fixed the value of α at 45°, from which it appears that there will be a slight balance against the nut, but this may easily be overcome by making the base of the nut slightly conical, so as to use the strength of the plate to resist splitting.

The proportions shown in the drawing, Fig. 4, Plate XXIV, are believed to be as near correct as they can be made with the available data.

The angle at the base of the nut is made equal to $(\alpha - 2\beta)$ or 45° — 18° = 27°. Since this angle has the same effect as an equal increase of the angle of friction, in preventing the nut from being forced outward, we must add it to the angle of friction (β) in equation (12,) the second member of which would become R^2. T. $\tan [\alpha - (2\beta + 27°)]$ and, since $\alpha = 2\beta - 27°$ by construction, this expression becomes equal to zero. In other words, there would be no tendency whatever for the nut to split, since the friction and oblique base would just equal the rupturing strain due to the wedging of the thread.

PROJECTILES.

The intimate connection between armor-plating and the means of destroying it, suggested a few experiments with projectiles of different forms and materials. Several of those tested are illustrated on Plate III, and the effect of firing, upon the shot itself, is shown for several particular cases on Plates IV and V.

Conclusions.—1st. Steel is the best material for shot, especially where penetration is desired. Chilled iron has been strongly advocated in Europe, and may do tolerably well for *pointed* shot, which expend their work gradually, but for flat-headed ones it would probably be very little better than ordinary cast iron. Captain Noble says in regard to chilled shot, (page 36 of the report already referred to:) "When the projectile can perforate with ease, the chilled shot is more formidable than steel, as it enters the ship broken up and would act as grape." If this be the case when the plate is perforated "with ease," what would take place when great resistance was met with! This appears to be a good argument *against* chilled shot. It must be admitted, however, that the chilled shot of Palliser in England, and of Grüson in Prussia, have given good results, especially when we consider the cheapness of the material.

2nd. In order to get a maximum effect, steel should be properly hardened. The difficulty of accomplishing this on a large scale is so great that it has not been generally carried out; and this fact may account for the preference given by some to the chilled shot. It is generally found in hardening large masses of steel, that the surface only is hardened, and that there is a strong tendency to crack at the center; but this may be obviated by forging the shot hollow, as will be mentioned elsewhere. Several examples of the great loss of work from the upsetting of unhardened shot were met with in these experiments. Figs. 5 and 6, Plate IV, show a hardened shot which perforated one inch of good wrought iron, and an unhardened one of the same description, which only made an indent one-eighth of an inch deep, both being fired with the same charge. Fig. 11, Plate V, shows an unhardened shot which penetrated only about one-eighth of an inch, when it should have gone through a ⅞-inch plate. It should be recollected, however, that the work done upon the plate by the unhardened shot was not as much smaller than that done by the hardened ones as the penetration was less than the thickness of the plate, since either of these shot, had they penetrated a little deeper, would have punched a plug out of the plate.

3rd. With uniform charges of 300 grains of powder, the penetrating powers of the different kinds of shot in good wrought iron were as follows, the plate being at right angles to the axis of the gun, and within six feet of the muzzle:

Fig. 1. Plate III: *Spherical shot* was just stopped by a $\frac{1}{2}$-inch plate.

Fig. 2, Plate III: *Cylindro-spherical* went through $\frac{5}{8}$-inch but not $\frac{3}{4}$-inch.

Fig. 3, Plate III: *Ogival*, a little better, though not through $\frac{3}{4}$-inch.

Fig. 4, Plate III: *Cylindrical*, through $\frac{3}{4}$-inch, and sometimes $\frac{7}{8}$-inch.

Fig. 5, Plate III: *Cylindrical hollow shot*—penetrating power about the same as with the last-mentioned form, but is thought to possess advantages in other respects, which will be mentioned in another place.

Fig. 6, Plate III: *Compound shot*, (of hardened steel and cast iron,) broke up, as shown in Fig. 2, Plate IV.

Fig. 7, Plate III: *Cylindro-cylindrical*—penetration considerably retarded by the projection in front, with no compensating advantages.

Fig. 8, Plate III: *Sub-caliber shot*—good for one inch of iron, and probably more.

Another form of *Ogival shot* was tested, the radius of the head being equal to two diameters of the shot, but the penetrating power was not perceptibly greater than that of the ogival shot already mentioned.

A spherical shot of soft lead perforated a plate $\frac{1}{4}$-inch thick, and another went very nearly through a $\frac{3}{8}$-inch plate. These shot were of the same diameter as the other spherical shot, and weighed 1,450 grains.

4th. When the impact is oblique the advantage of the cylindrical, or flat-headed form, is still more decided, as will be seen from the account of experiments on oblique impact.

5th. With regard to the damage sustained by the shot themselves, it was found that the ogival ones stood best, and the cylindrical ones worst; the former being often fired six or eight times over without perceptible injury, while the latter were seldom fired more than once without being so much distorted, or upset, as not to go into the gun.

6th. The hole made by the flat-headed shot, especially in laminated plating, is larger and more ragged, and the concussion is greater than with any other form of projectile of equal diameter.

7th. At long range the flat-headed shot would, of course, lose more from resistance of the air than either of the other forms.

Pointed, vs. Flat-headed Shot.

As the foregoing conclusions differ somewhat from those given in Captain Noble's report, already referred to, some explanation may not be out of place; the more important of these differences being in regard to the relative advantages of the ogival and cylindrical, or pointed and flat-headed projectiles.

The reason urged in favor of pointed shot, in the report just referred to, is that, having got through the iron, the *ogival shot* meets with less resistance in penetrating the wooden backing. This is evidently the case. But it must be admitted that the first thing to be done is to *get through the iron*, especially since it has been found practicable to use armor-plating without any wooden backing at all; and it is therefore important that no means of getting through the iron should be omitted for the purpose of increasing the penetration in wood. If one shot will go through the plating, with ever so little remaining velocity, the chances of doing damage must necessarily be greater than from another shot which fails to get through at all; provided, of course, that penetration is the object in view. If, on the other hand, smashing effect is desired, the spherical shot would be better than either of those under consideration.

The manner in which the work is expended in case of flat-headed shot, is represented in Figs. 1 and 2, Plate XXII. The resistance is a maximum soon after the penetration begins, and continues nearly constant for a short distance, (about one-fifth of the thickness of the plate,) when the plate begins to split laterally, and the resistance to diminish rapidly, until the plug is forced through the opening.

The curves, Nos. 1 and 4, represent the resistances at the different points of the penetration: and, in each case, the area bounded by the curve, the axis of the shot, and the front of the plate is a measure for the work of perforation. Curves Nos. 2 and 5 indicate the same for the ogival shot.

The resistance is zero when the point of the shot first touches the plate. It then increases until the hole is the full size of the shot, or, depending upon the thickness of the plate, until the point of the shot begins to break through the back of the plate. It then begins to diminish, and this diminution continues until the largest part of the shot nearly or quite reaches the rear surface of the plate, at which point the resistance ceases.

The areas of the curves which represent the work, as before mentioned, are, in this case, more than twice as great as in the case of the flat-headed shot.

These curves were constructed by punching the shot through the plate in a testing machine—the penetration and corresponding resistance being measured at successive points.

The foregoing results were corroborated by observing the effects of both kinds of shot fired at plates of different thicknesses, some shot getting through and others being stopped at different stages of the penetration. Some of the same plates were put in a testing machine and the same shot were forced through them by a steady pressure, the resistance being measured for regular increments of penetration. The results of some of these tests are shown in the diagrams, (Fig. 3, Plate XXII,) the dotted lines representing the theoretical, and the full ones the actual resistances. A ring about 2½ inches in diameter was placed under the plates instead of the die used in ordinary punching, in order to allow the fracture to take place as nearly as possible like that produced by firing the shot through the same plates; and this was very satisfactorily accomplished. The fracture and plug punched out was almost identical with those produced by the impact of the shot in firing. In the case of Nos. 4 and 5, Fig. 2, the ring was a little smaller, which increased the resistance about 12,000 pounds in each case, but without materially changing the relative amount of work in the two cases.

That the curves do not come down to the axis as soon as the dotted lines is due to the friction between the shot and plate, which does not probably take place to the same extent when the shot are moving at high velocities, as they then have a better chance to clear themselves.

It was found by firing into lead that a shot not only clears itself but makes a hole considerably larger than its own diameter, (Rounds 334 and 335, Plate XVIII,) and in iron the hole is generally large enough for the shot to slip through freely, provided it has gone through with some remaining velocity.

A still further comparison of the two methods of punching is represented in Fig. 3, Plate XXII.

Three shot, (Rounds 165, 167, and 211,) were fired at an inch plate, and having failed to get through, were punched the remaining distance in the testing machine. The 165th and 167th rounds were cylindrical and were fired with 350 grains of powder; the 211th was ogival and fired with a 500-grain charge.

From these results it will be seen that it makes but little difference whether a shot is fired part way and punched the rest, or punched the whole distance, as far as the amount of work is concerned. It also appears that the work of punching a flat-headed shot through an inch plate, after it has penetrated about ⅞ of an inch, is less than it is to punch an ogival shot through after the point has entirely perforated the plate.

This last round, the 211th, was fired with a charge of 500 grains, and a velocity of about 1,140 feet. The work was, therefore, in round numbers, 9,000 foot-pounds. The work of punching the same shot to the same distance in the same plate, as measured by the testing machine, was about 6,000 foot-pounds. This leaves 3,000 foot-pounds, or one-third of the whole work of the shot for bending the plate, upsetting the shot, generating heat, and other losses of work which are known to occur under these circumstances.

No. 3 was punched in from the beginning, in the same manner as Nos. 2 and 5, (Figs. 1 and 2,) and with similar results.

There were quite a number of facts developed in these experiments, tending to show that the curves given very nearly represent what actually takes place when the shot is fired through the plate; but it is not thought worth while to devote more space to the subject, until a number of additional experiments have been made, so as to obtain more accurate results.

Returning to the relative advantages of flat-headed and pointed shot, the tendency to "upset" is greater in case of the flat-headed than in that of the pointed shot, and, in fact, than almost any other form; and this is probably one of the reasons why they have not given better results in large experiments.

The flat-head expends its work suddenly, while the pointed shot stops more gradually and meets its greatest resistance after its velocity has been considerably reduced.

The question is, then, whether it is better to stop the shot gradually, for fear of breaking it, or let it take its chances with the target.

If cast iron, wrought iron, or soft steel, are to be the materials from which the shot are made, this question may be answered in the affirmative; but if hardened steel is used, there is at least a strong probability in favor of the flat-headed shot.

The pointed shot has a decided advantage in punching targets which are so constructed that the shot may wedge its way *between* the bars or plates, and where the hole is so near the edge as to break out; but where a hole must be made through solid metal, it had better be done by cutting the full size at once, as is done by the flat-headed cylindrical shot.

Many shot have been tried, as the Whitworth, Parrott, and Brooke shot, having a flat head, but smaller than the shot, the effect being to punch a hole too small at first and leaving a great amount of work to be done by the rear part of the shot in forcing its way through.

The shot used in nearly all the large experiments have, as before stated, been considerably upset or broken in pieces, and it has been found impossible until quite recently to get a shot through its own thickness of solid wrought iron.

Possible Improvements in Projectiles.

Since armor-plating is for *future*, rather than present, use, it becomes an important question whether the limit to the penetrating power of projectiles, of a given diameter, has been reached, and, if not, how that power can be increased.

It is not presumed that these experiments, or any amount of theorizing upon them, can settle such questions as these definitely; but they may indicate certain contingencies which should be duly considered in determining the safe thickness for armor-plating.

In the first place, the effect of hardening shot is probably much greater than is generally supposed. That is, the amount of work gained is much greater than the increase in strength of the shot.

It is well known that a very small force may, under certain circumstances, determine the performance or non-performance of a very large amount of *work*. Take for illustration a heavy vertical piston, P, (Fig. 1, Plate XXIV,) fitting friction-tight in a socket S, and sustaining, also by friction, the collar C. Let now a very small weight, W, be placed upon the top of the piston, and the piston, collar, and weight will fall through the distance *d*, and the work done will be $(P+C+W)\times d$. But let the same weight be placed upon the collar, so as not to bear directly upon the piston, and the fall will be the same, but only the collar and weight will move, and the work will be $(C+W)\times d$.

This result being entirely independent of the relative weights of P, C, and W, we may have $P=100{,}000$ pounds, $C=10$ pounds, $W=1$ pound, and $d=10$ feet. The work would then be in the first case 1,000,110 foot-pounds, and in the second only 110 foot-pounds, the difference being due entirely to changing the one-pound weight.

In like manner, a very slight addition to the rigidity of a shot, by hardening or otherwise, may determine whether a very large amount of work shall be wasted upon the shot or expended upon the plate. For example, a sub-caliber shot, not hardened, was upset one-sixth of its length, and penetrated only one-eighth inch, while a similar shot which was hardened full length, and which struck with the same velocity, made a clean hole through an inch of solid metal. (Figs. 5 and 6, Plate IV.) I have never heard of any experiments with properly hardened steel shot of large size, and presume the reason for their not having been used has been the difficulty of hardening large masses of steel without producing cracks or at least strains, which would weaken rather than strengthen the shot.

In order to overcome this difficulty, the hollow shot (Fig. 5, Plate III) was devised, the hole through the center allowing the sudden shrinkage to take place without the injurious effects alluded to. That this was accomplished was shown by the fact that several shot, made in this manner, were so little injured by firing that they were fired a second time, which was rarely the case with the solid ones of the same form and weight.

It was also found that shot of this form penetrated the plate easier on account of the middle portion being relieved from the pressure met with by solid shot. The 69th and 70th rounds (Figs. 3 and 4, Plate IV) showed that the larger the hole through the shot the easier it went through the plate.

Another advantage secured by making shot of this form, is, that in forging, the metal may be compressed from the center outwards, and thus avoid a well-known practical difficulty in forging large masses of steel, when hammered upon the outside only. It may also be mentioned, by way of disposing of the subject, that the hole through this shot was made larger at the rear in order to throw the center of gravity forward of the center of figure, and thus prevent "tumbling" when little or no rifle motion is given.

A second means of increasing the work done upon the plate, in comparison with that done upon the shot, is by increasing the velocity of the latter. That is, a shot moving at a low velocity may be smashed up or flattened against a plate, while the same shot fired at a higher velocity may go through the same plate almost uninjured. On this principle a lead shot may be fired through an iron plate, or a tallow candle through a pine board.

Among the plans for increasing the velocity of projectiles, the two following are worthy of notice:

(*a*) The accelerating principle, or a number of chambers or pockets along the barrel, containing separate charges of powder, to be ignited as the shot passes them in succession. This is known as Lyman's gun; and,

(*b*) The enlarged chamber for the powder, so as to use a very large charge with a small caliber of gun. It is reported that the Ferris gun, on this principle, has given an initial velocity of 2,200 feet, and a range of *nine miles*. The gun was, however, a small one, the shot weighing only 3¾ pounds, and the charge 12½ pounds.

The Merriam gun, similar in principle, has given a corresponding velocity and the greatest penetration on record for a musket, viz: 16 inches in solid oak, besides several thicknesses of pine boards. The application of these principles to large cannon is, however, as yet extremely problematical.

Thirdly, the penetration may be increased by diminishing the diameter of the shot, without reducing the surface acted upon by the gas in giving it velocity, as is accomplished by the sub-caliber shot of Stafford and others, the principle being essentially the same as in the small sub-caliber shot already mentioned.

There is good reason to believe that a projectile of this kind may be adapted to the 15-inch gun, to operate without rotary motion, and such a projectile, with the service charge of powder, would probably find its way through 16 or 18 inches of wrought iron; and a similar arrangement for the 20-inch gun would, under the same supposition, perforate say 24 inches. Of course this is mere conjecture, but it involves no change whatever in the service guns, charges, or velocities; and there appears to be no mechanical impossibility in the way of the fabrication and use of the projectiles.

PLATES AND TABLES.

The following plates and tables, representing some of the apparatus used and results attained in these experiments, will be readily understood without further explanation.

The *plates*, with the exception of Fig. 3, Plate I, and Fig. 1, Plate II, which are in perspective, were drawn to a scale either directly from the objects or from their photographs and dimensions.

In those cases where it appeared desirable to show the effect upon the rear of the target, it will be found upon the back of the same sheet, covering the front view of the target.

The *tables* give the weight of the charge of powder used in each case, but not the velocity nor the work of the shot. The mean velocities and work due to the different charges were as follows:

Spherical Shot.

Weight of charge.	Velocity.	Work.
300 grains.	1,230 feet.	3,503 foot-pounds.
350 grains.	1,294 feet.	3,877 foot-pounds.
400 grains.	1,354 feet.	4,245 foot-pounds.

Elongated Shot.

Weight of charge.	Velocity.	Work.
300 grains.	920 feet.	5,853 foot-pounds.
350 grains.	985 feet.	6,709 foot-pounds.
400 grains.	1,040 feet.	7,479 foot-pounds.
500 grains.	1,140 feet.	8,987 foot-pounds.

APPARATUS.

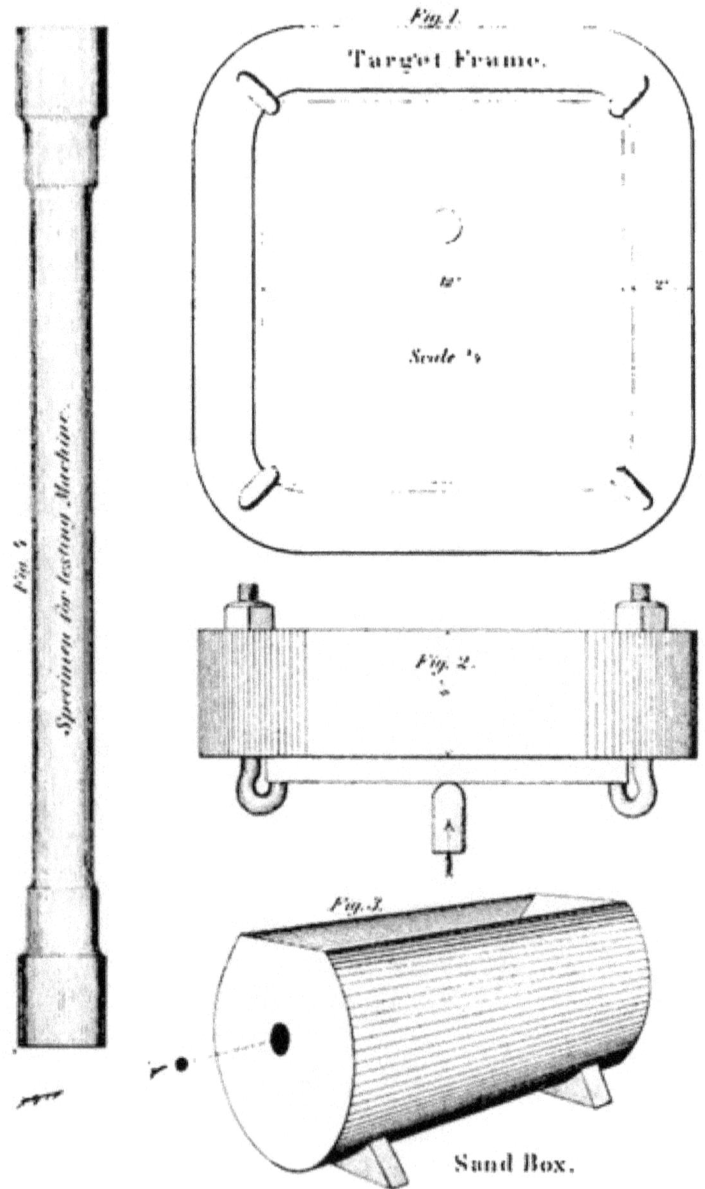

Fig. 1.
Target Frame.
Scale
Fig. 2.
Fig. 3.
Sand Box.
Specimen for testing Machine.

PLATE II.

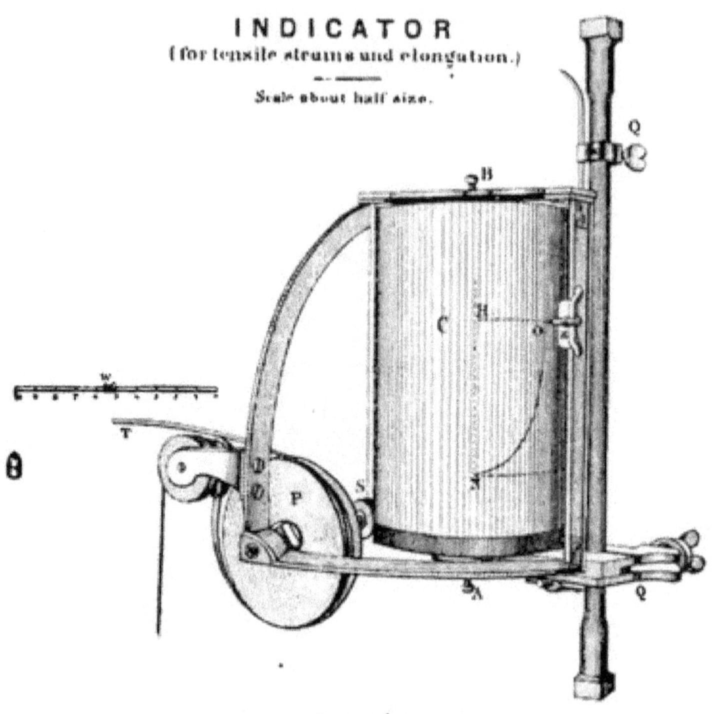

Common form of Specimen
for tensile strenght.
Full Size.

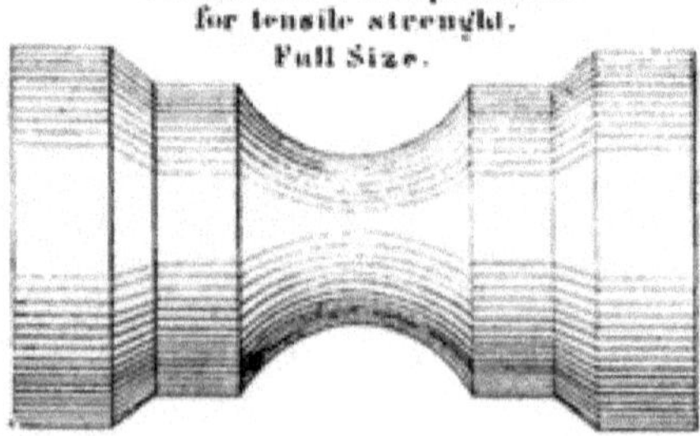

PLATE III.

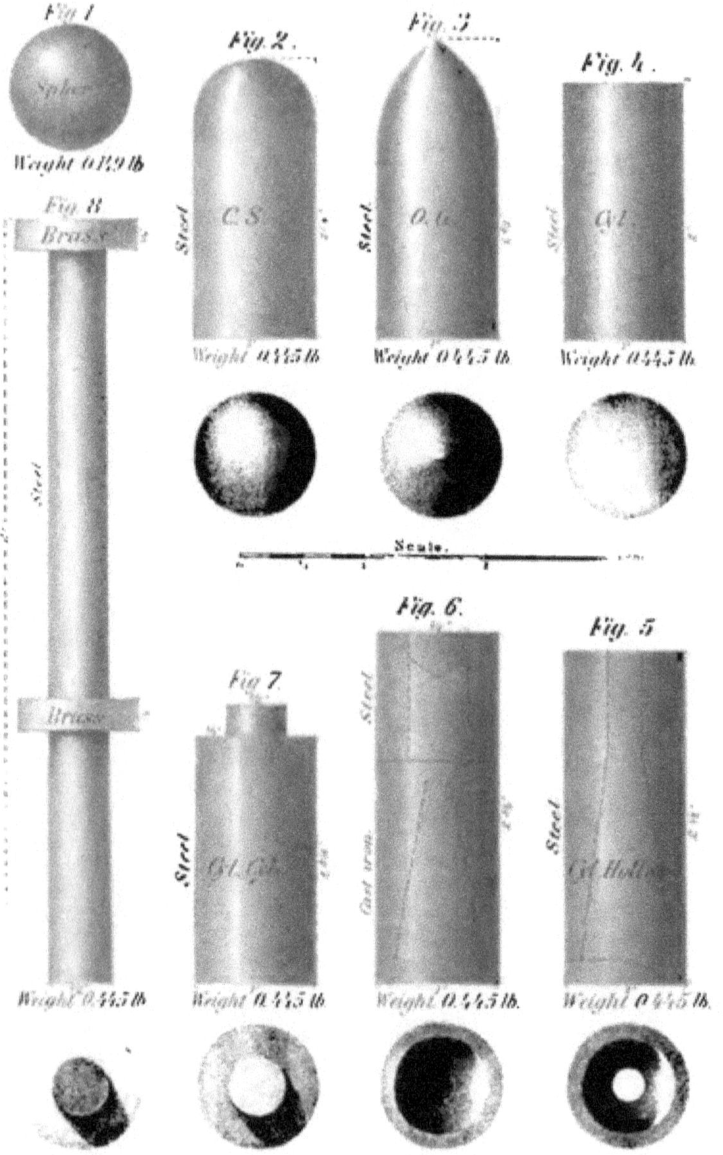
SHOT (before firing.)
Fig. 1
Weight 0.129 lb
Fig. 2.
Steel
C.S.
Weight 0.445 lb
Fig. 3
Steel
Weight 0.445 lb.
Fig. 4.
Weight 0.445 lb.
Fig. 8
Weight 0.445 lb
Scale.
Fig. 6.
Steel
Weight 0.445 lb.
Fig. 5
Steel
Weight 0.445 lb.
Fig. 7
Steel
Weight 0.445 lb.

PLATE IV.

SHOT (after firing)

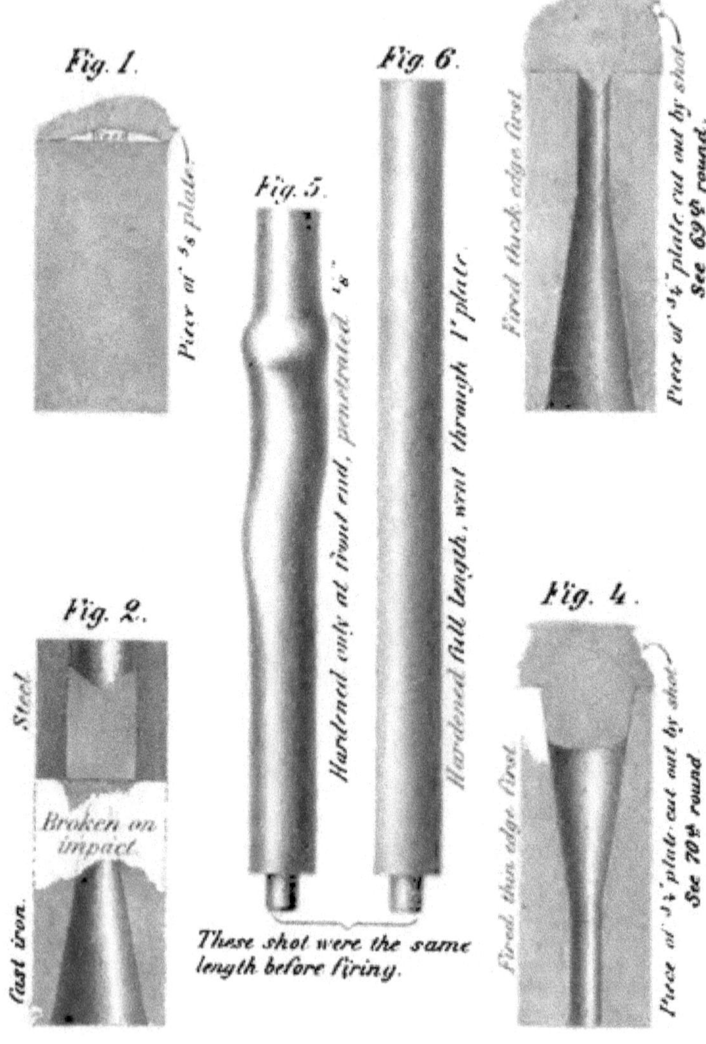

Fig. 1.
Piece of ⅝" plate
Fig. 2.
Steel
Broken on impact
Cast iron.
Fig. 5.
Hardened only at front end, penetrated ⅛"
Fig. 6.
Hardened full length, went through 1" plate.
These shot were the same length before firing.
Fig. 3.
Fired thick edge first
Piece of ¾" plate cut out by shot
See 69th round.
Fig. 4.
Fired thin edge first
Piece of ¾" plate cut out by shot
See 70th round
Scale

PLATE V.

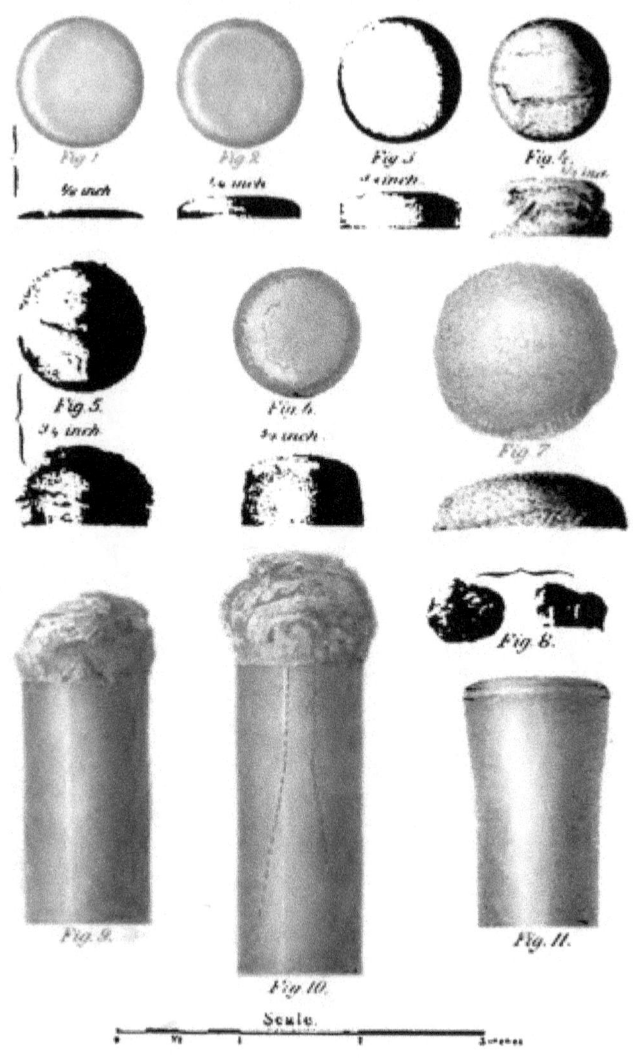
SHOT (after firing) and
pieces of plate punched out.
Fig. 1
Fig. 2
Fig. 3
Fig. 4
Fig. 5
Fig. 6
Fig. 7
Fig. 8
Fig. 9
Fig. 10
Fig. 11
Scale.

TABLE VI.

No. of round.	Thickness of plate.	Weight of charge.	Form of shot. (*See Plate III.*)	Penetration, &c. (*Deepest point.*)
160	¾ inch.	300 grains.	Ogival.	1 inch.
161	¾ inch.	300 grains.	Cylindrical.	Clean hole.
162	¾ inch.	300 grains.	Ogival.	15-16 inch.
163	¾ inch.	300 grains.	Ogival.	⅞ inch.
164	1 inch.	300 grains.	Cylindrical.	7-16 inch.
165	1 inch.	350 grains.	Cylindrical.	⅜ inch.
166	1 inch.	350 grains.	Cylindrical.	⅜ inch.
167	1 inch.	350 grains.	Cylindrical.	7-16 inch.
168	1 inch.	400 grains.	Cylindrical.	⅝ inch.
169	1 inch.	300 grains.	Sub-calibre.	Clean hole.
170	1 inch.	340 grains.	Cylindrical-hollow.	Not through.
171	1 inch.	300 grains.	Sub-calibre.	Shot broke in half
172	1 inch.	300 grains.	Sub-calibre.	11-16 inch. Shot upset
173	1 inch.	400 grains.	Cylindrical-hollow.	7-16 inch. Shot crumbled
174	1 inch.	400 grains.	Cylindrical-hollow.	Almost through.
175	1 inch.	300 grains.	Cylindro-spherical.	11-16 inch.
176	1 inch.	400 grains.	Cylindro-spherical.	⅞ inch.
177	1 inch.	300 grains.	Ogival.	9-16 inch.
178	1 inch.	300 grains.	Ogival.	13-16 inch.
179	1 inch.	300 grains.	Ogival.	11-16 inch.
180	1 inch.	300 grains.	Cylindro-spherical.	⅞ inch.

[NOTE.] 1. See "Solid Plating" and "Projectiles."
2. The "following plate" is on the back of same sheet.

WROUGHT IRON.

(See following plate)

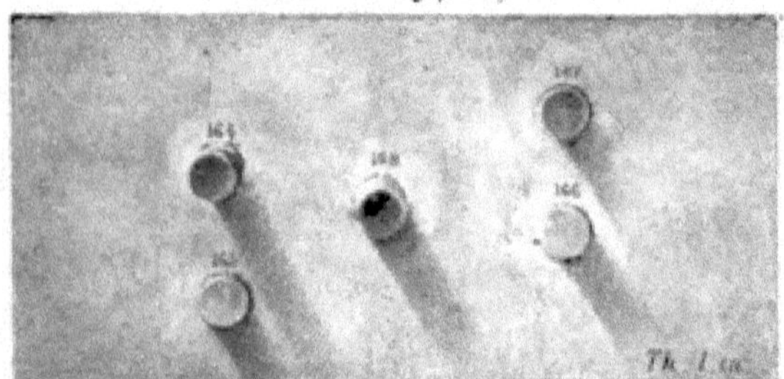

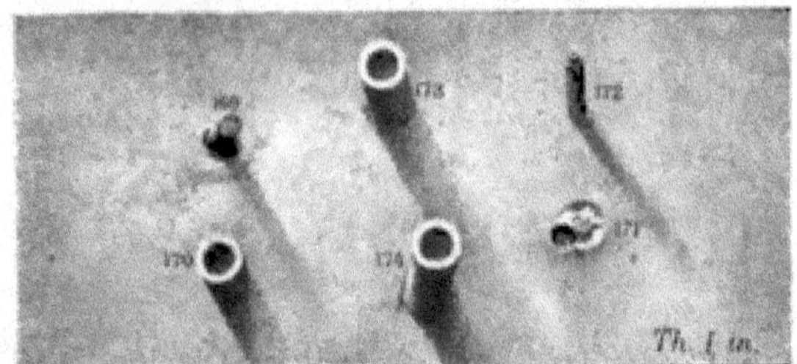

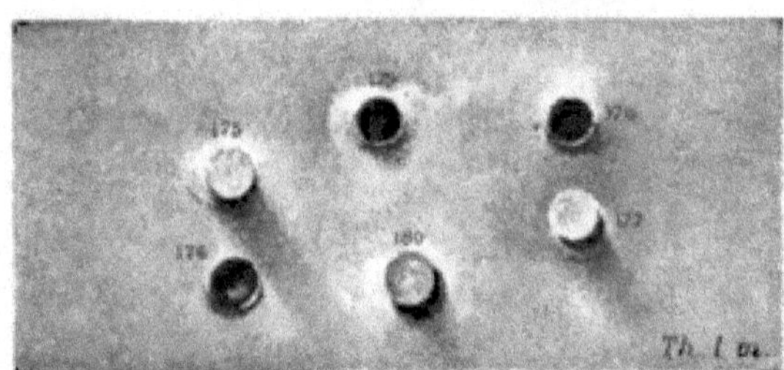

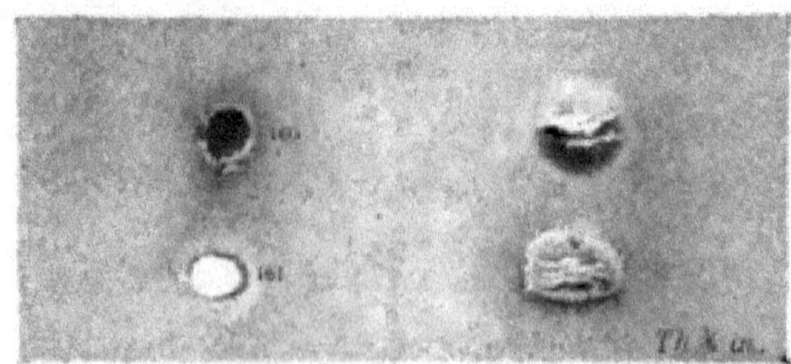

(See preceding plate.)

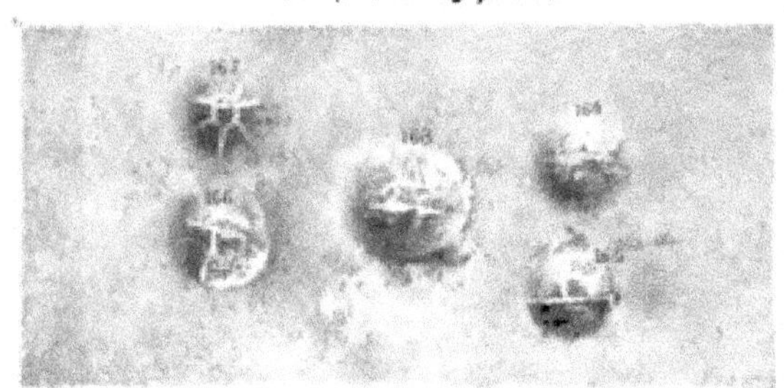

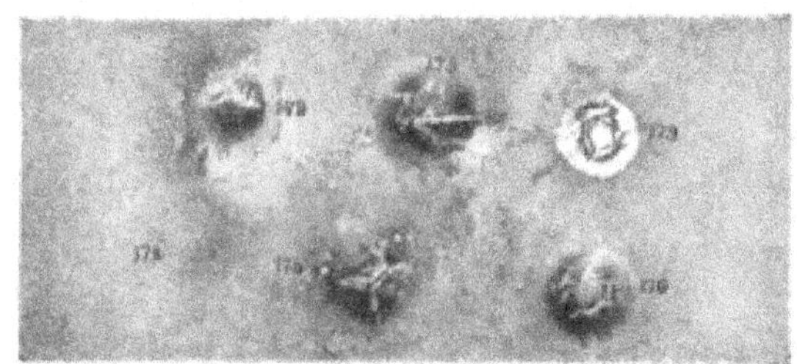

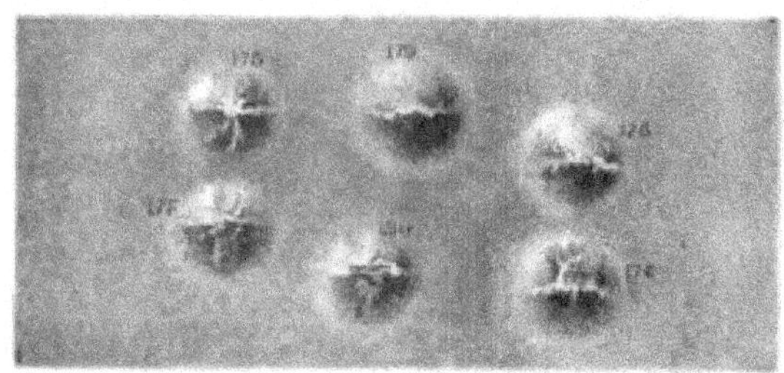

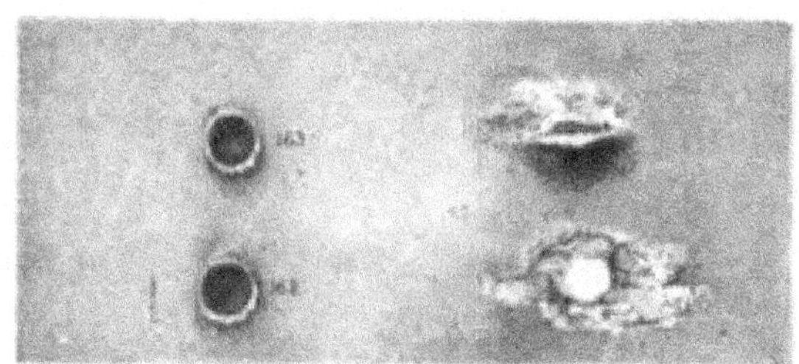

TABLE VII.

No. of round.	Thickness of plate.	Weight of charge.	Form of shot. (*See Plate III.*)	Penetration, &c. (*Deepest point.*)
195	¼ inch.	350 grains.	Cylindro-spherical.	Clean hole.
196	¼ inch.	350 grains.	Cylindro-spherical.	Point through.
197	¼ inch.	350 grains.	Ogival.	Point through.
198	¼ inch.	350 grains.	Ogival.	Point through.
199	¼ inch.	350 grains.	Cylindro-spherical.	Just through.
200	¼ inch.	350 grains.	Ogival.	Point through.
204	1 inch.	500 grains.	Cylindrical.	⅜ inch. Shot broken.
205	1 inch.	500 grains.	Cylindrical.	Just through.
207	1 inch.	500 grains.	Cylindrical.	Clean hole.
208	1 inch.	500 grains.	Cylindrical.	⅜ inch. Shot upset.
209	1 inch.	500 grains.	Cylindrical.	Through.
210	1 inch.	500 grains.	Ogival.	1 inch.
211	1 inch.	500 grains.	Ogival.	17-16 inch.
212	1 inch.	500 grains.	Cylindro-spherical.	⅜ inch.
213	1 inch.	500 grains.	Cylindro-spherical.	⅜ inch.

[NOTE.] See "Solid Plating" and "Projectiles."

WROUGHT IRON.

(See following plate)

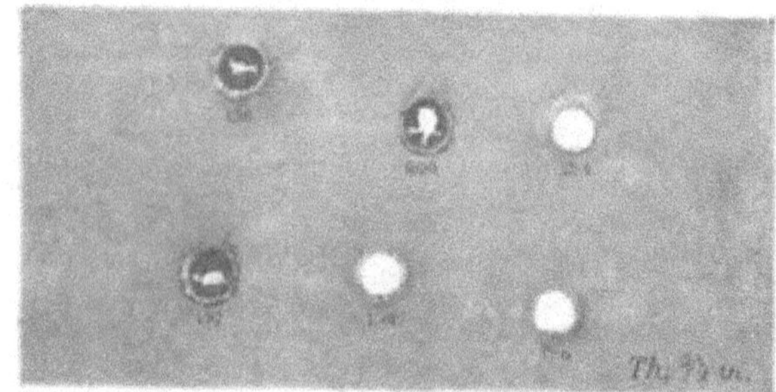

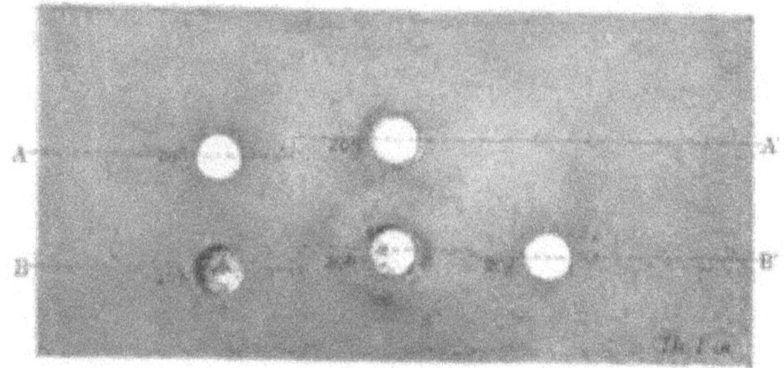

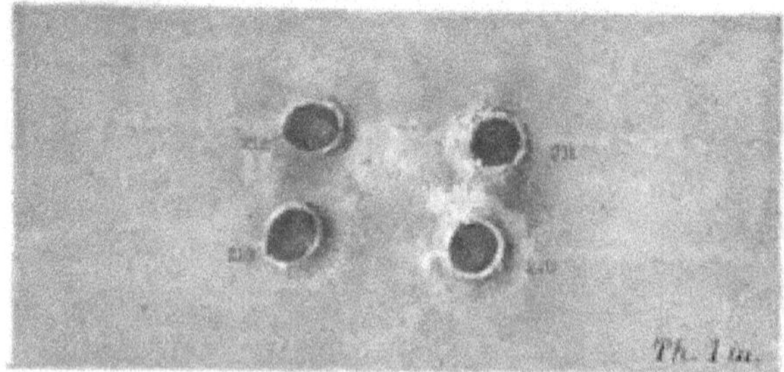

(See preceding plate.)

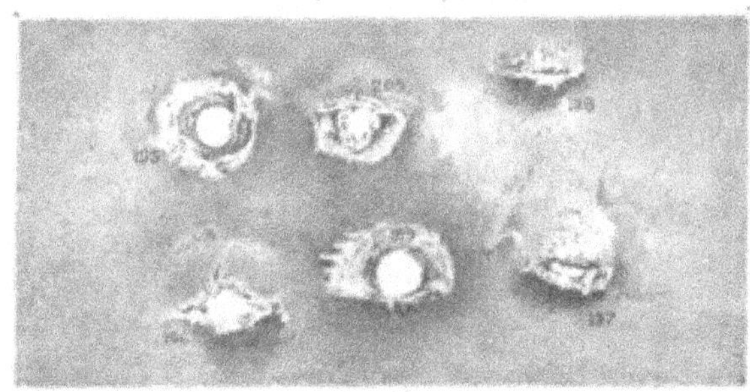

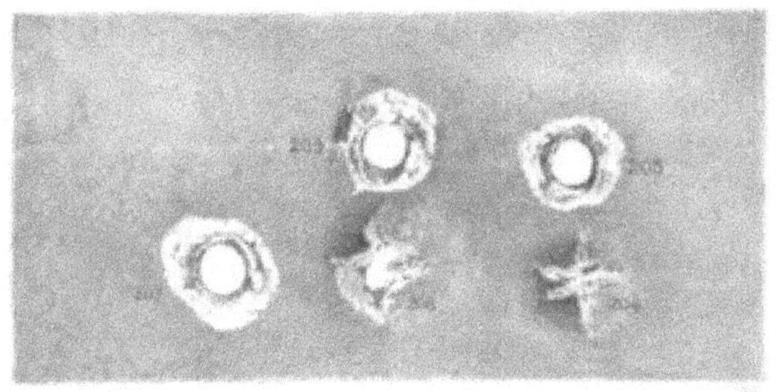

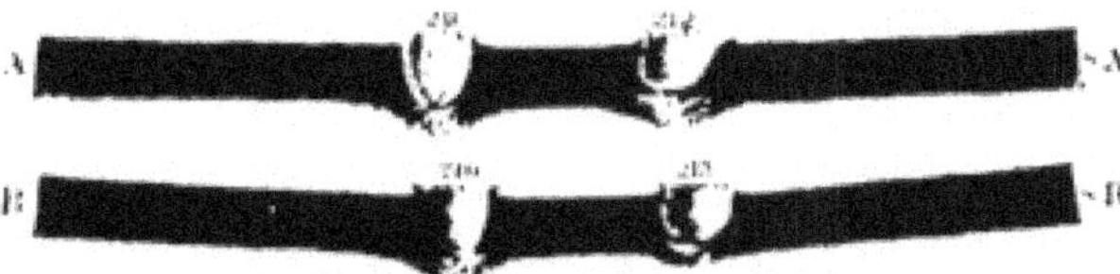

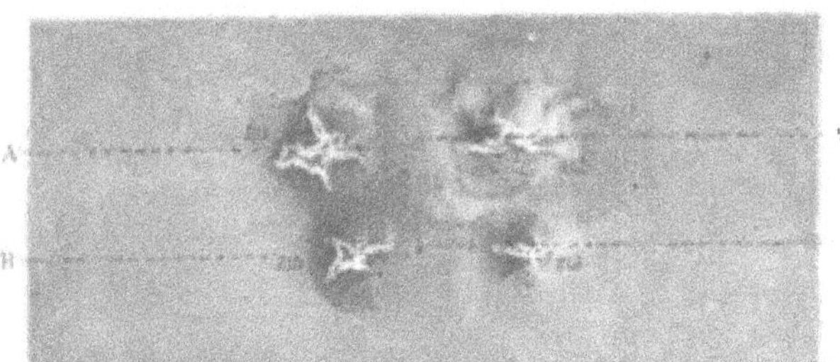

TABLE VIII.

No. of round.	Thickness of plate.	Weight of charge.	Form of shot. (*See Plate III.*)	Penetration, &c. (*Deepest point.*)
411	Two [illegible]-inch.	300 grains.	Cylindrical.	Not quite through.
412	Two 3/8-inch.	300 grains.	Cylindrical.	Not quite through.
423	One [illegible]-inch.	300 grains.	Cylindrical.	Just through.
424	One [illegible]-inch.	300 grains.	Cylindrical.	Just through.
270	[illegible] inch.	300 grains.	Spherical.	Clean hole; common iron.
315	[illegible] inch.	300 grains.	Spherical.	Not quite through.
273	[illegible] inch.	300 grains.	Spherical.	Clean hole; Juniata iron.
316	[illegible] inch.	300 grains.	Spherical.	Not quite through; same plate annealed.
271	[illegible] inch.	300 grains.	Spherical.	7-16 inch; Lake Superior charcoal iron, refined.
318	[illegible] inch.	300 grains.	Spherical.	7-16 inch; same plate annealed.
295	[illegible] inch.	300 grains.	Spherical.	Almost through; Lake Superior charcoal iron.
296	5/8 inch.	300 grains.	Spherical.	Clean hole; Lake Superior charcoal iron.
294	[illegible] inch.	300 grains.	Spherical.	Clean hole; Lake Superior charcoal iron. (Not on plate.)
272	[illegible] inch.	300 grains.	Spherical.	Clean hole; Lake Superior charcoal iron. (Not on plate.)
317	[illegible] inch.	300 grains.	Spherical.	Not quite through; same plate annealed. (Not on plate.)

[NOTE.] See "Laminated Plating."

PLATE VIII.

WROUGHT IRON

(See following plate)

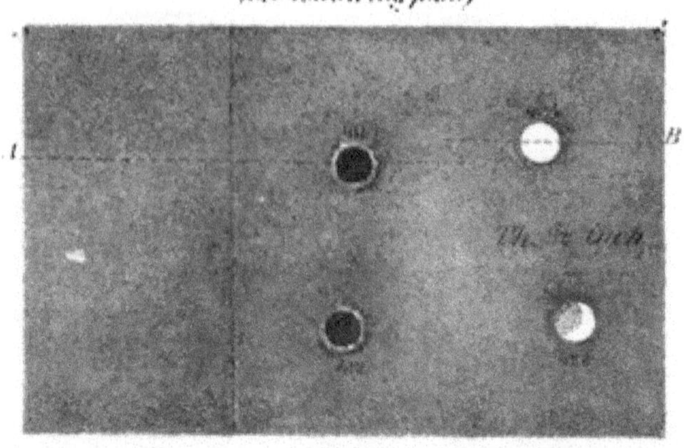

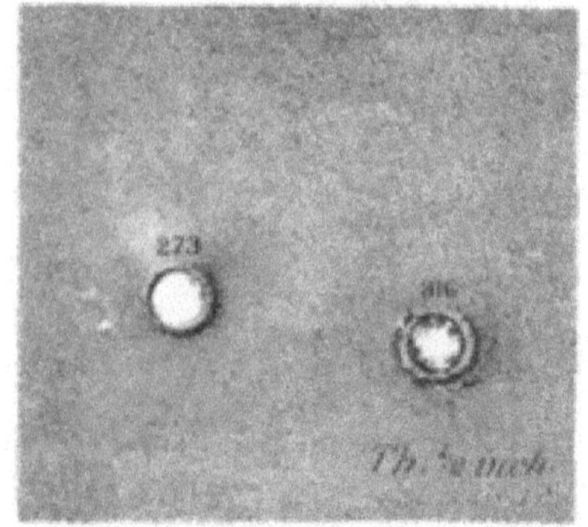

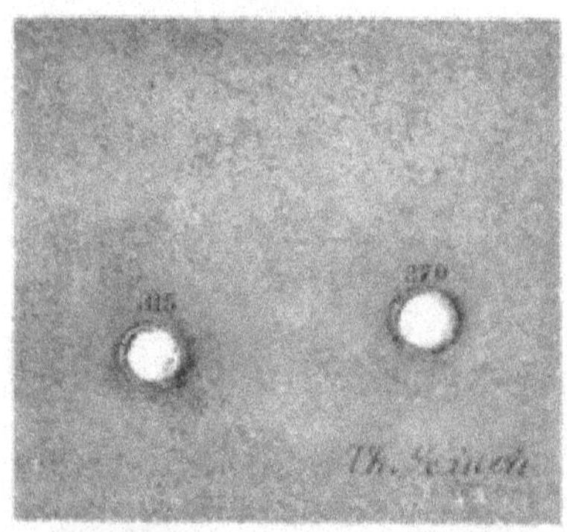

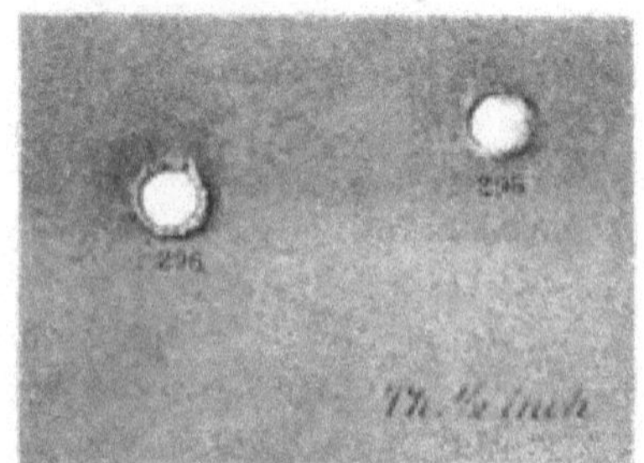

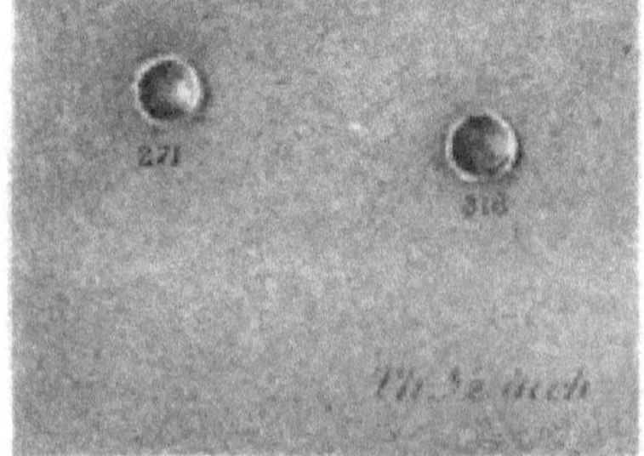

(See preceding plate.)

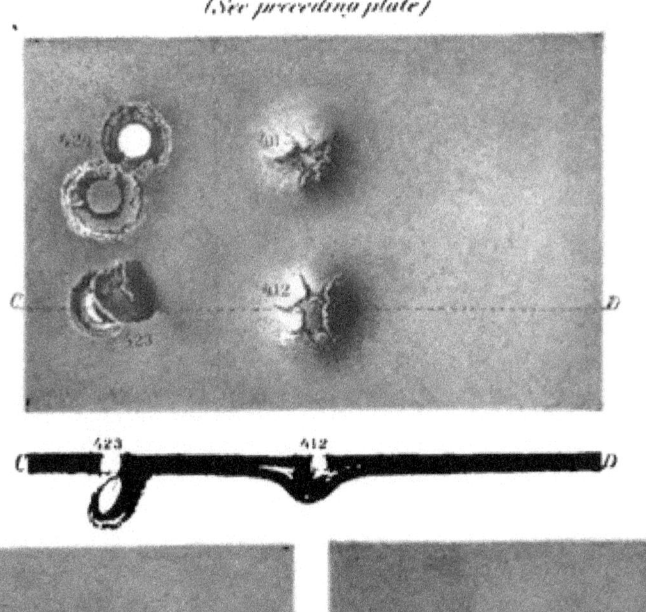

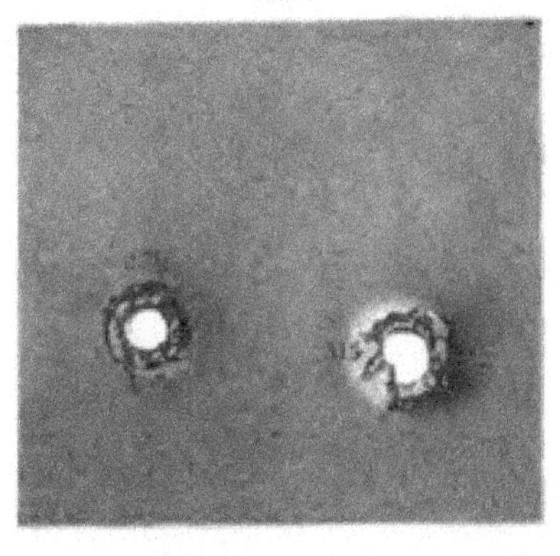

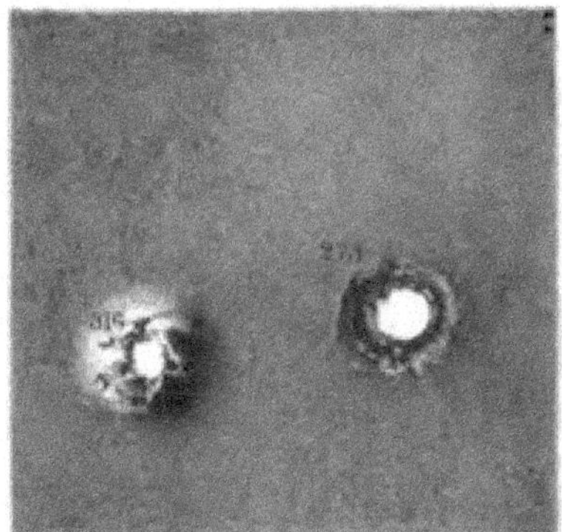

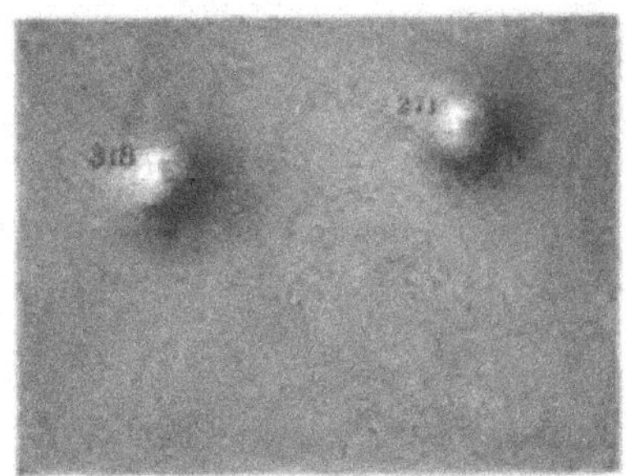

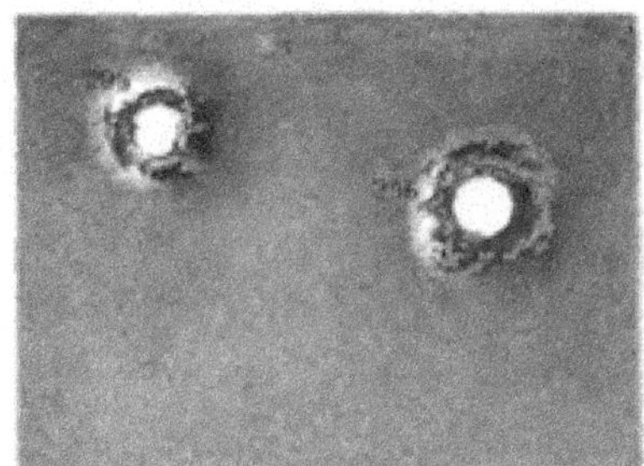

TABLE IX.

No. of round.	Thickness of plate.	Weight of charge.	Form of shot. (*See Plate III.*)	Penetration, &c. (*Deepest point.*)
5	[illegible] inch.	300 grains.	Spherical.	1 inch.
54	[illegible] inch.	300 grains.	Spherical.	[illegible] inch.
65	Two [illegible]-inch.	300 grains.	Spherical.	[illegible] inch.
66	Two [illegible]-inch.	300 grains.	Spherical.	[illegible] inch.
152	Two [illegible]-inch.	350 grains.	Spherical.	Through.
153	Two [illegible]-inch.	350 grains.	Spherical.	Through.
154	Two [illegible]-inch.	325 grains.	Spherical.	Through.
155	Two [illegible]-inch.	325 grains.	Spherical.	Through.
156	[illegible] inch.	325 grains.	Spherical.	Almost through.
157	[illegible] inch.	325 grains.	Spherical.	Almost through. Shot upset.
158	[illegible] inch.	325 grains.	Spherical.	Through.
159	[illegible] inch.	325 grains.	Spherical.	Through.
[illegible]	[illegible] inch.	300 grains.	Cylindrical.	Clean hole.
[illegible]	[illegible] inch.	300 grains.	Cylindrical.	Clean hole.
53	[illegible] inch.	300 grains.	Cylindrical-hollow.	Clean hole.
[illegible]	[illegible] inch.	350 grains.	Cylindro-spherical.	Clean hole.
[illegible]	Two [illegible]-inch.	300 grains.	Cylindrical.	Just through.
[illegible]	Two [illegible]-inch.	300 grains.	Cylindrical.	Not through.

[Note.] See "Laminated Plating."

WROUGHT IRON.

(See following plate.)

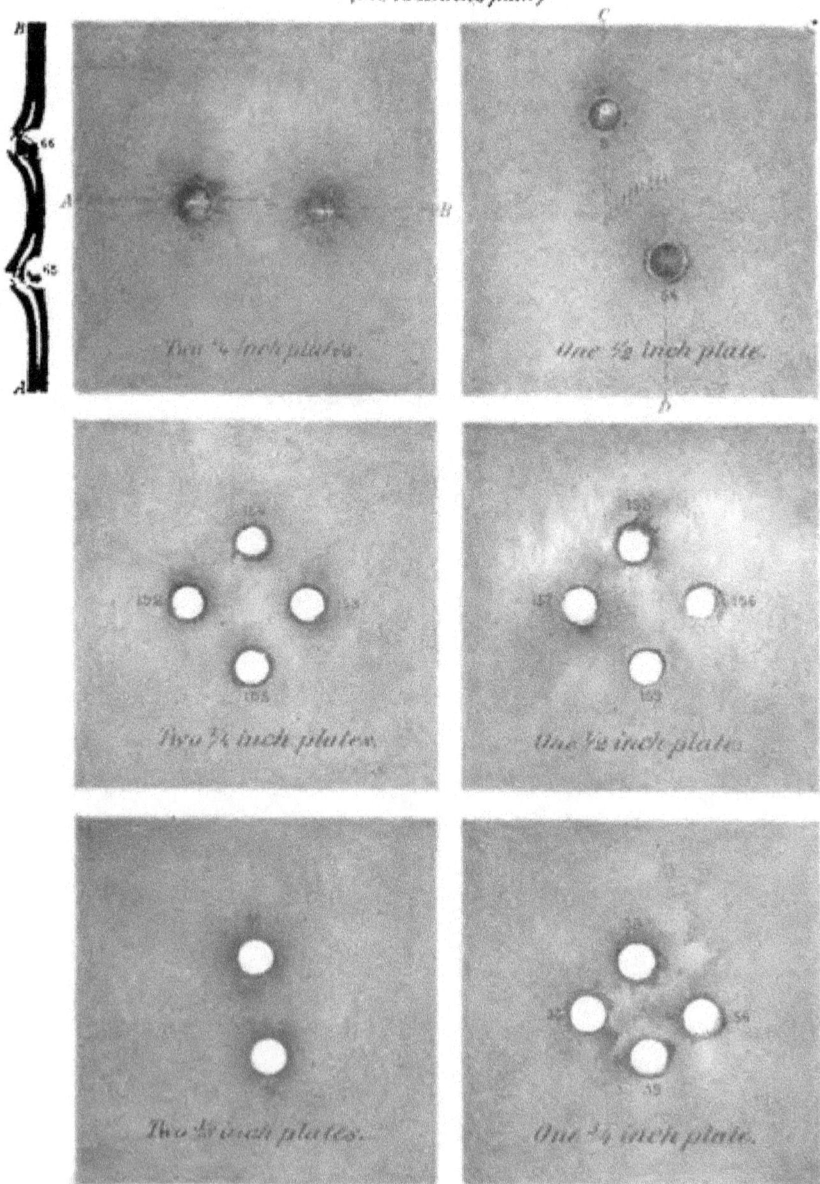

(See preceding plate)

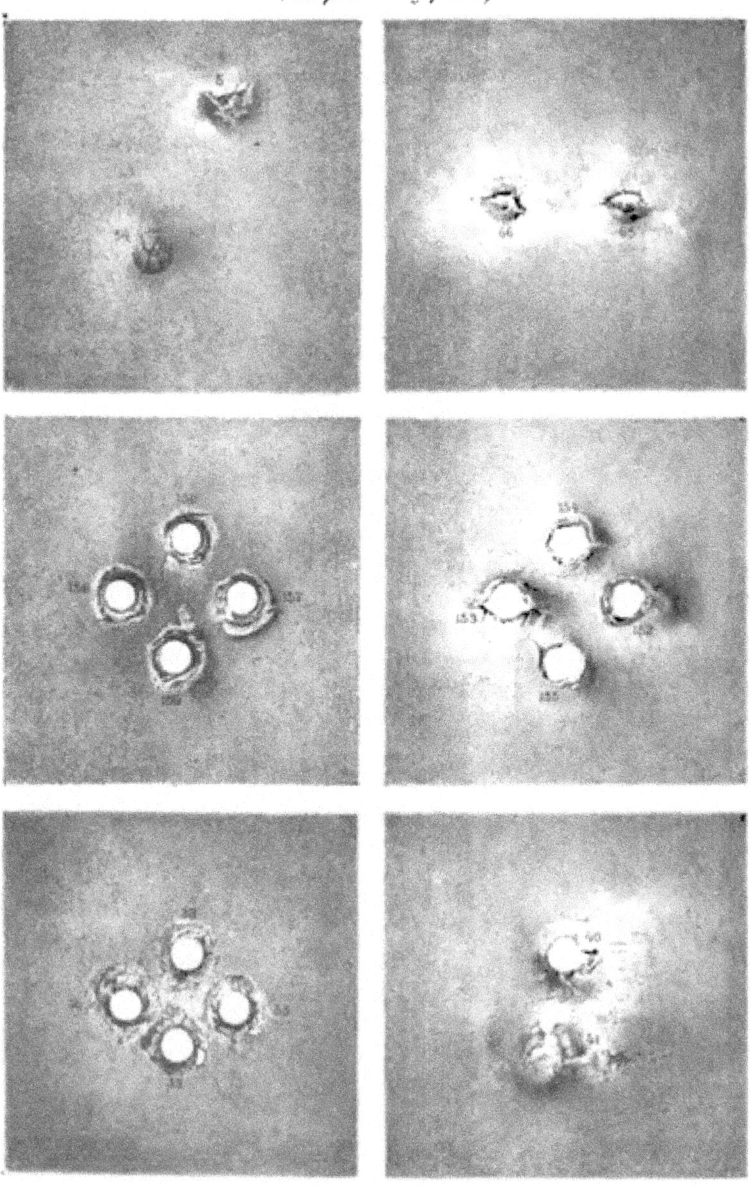

TABLE X.

No. of round.	Thickness of plate.	Weight of charge.	Form of shot. (*See Plate III.*)	Penetration, &c. (*Deepest point.*)
214	Six 1/8-in. plates.	300 grains.	Ogival.	Shot tumbled.
215	Six 1/8-in. plates.	300 grains.	Ogival.	Through.
216	Six 1/8-in. plates.	300 grains.	Ogival.	Through.
217	Six 1/8-in. plates.	300 grains.	Cylindro-spherical.	Through.
218	Seven 1/8-in. pl's.	300 grains.	Ogival.	Point just through third plate.
219	Seven 1/8-in. pl's.	300 grains.	Ogival.	Point just through third plate.
220	Seven 1/8-in. pl's.	300 grains.	Cylindrical.	Just through.
221	Seven 1/8-in. pl's.	300 grains.	Cylindrical.	Just through.

[NOTE.] See "Laminated Plating."

WROUGHT IRON.

(See following plate)

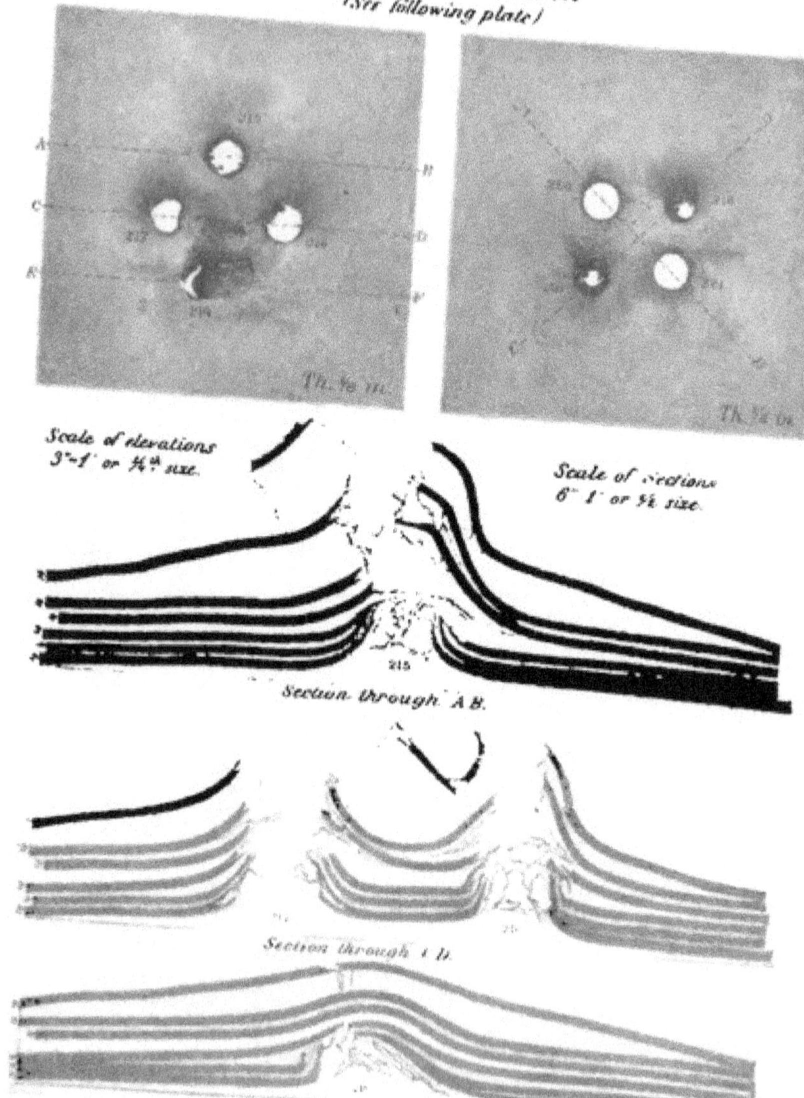

(See preceding plate)

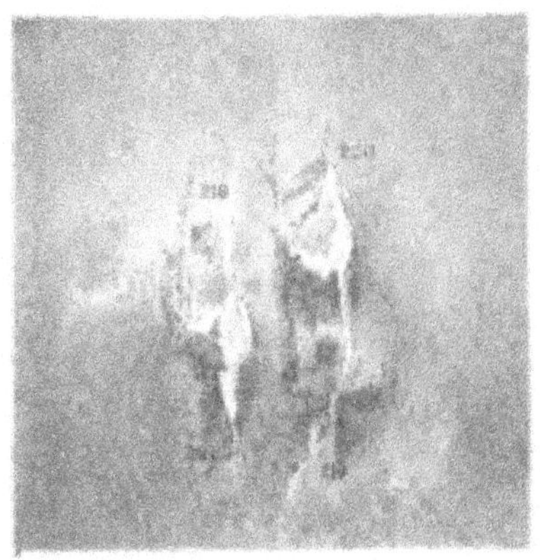

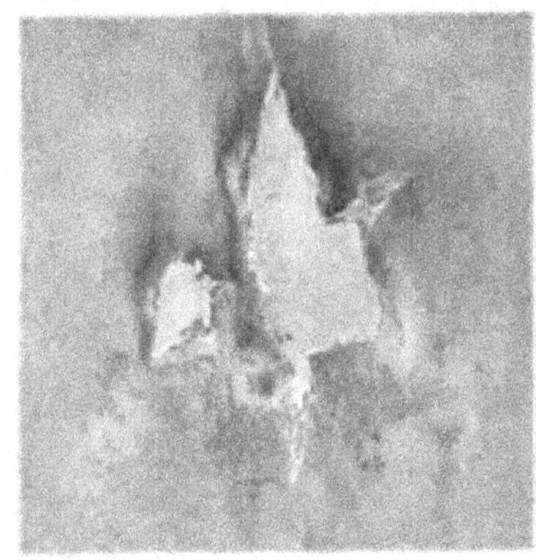

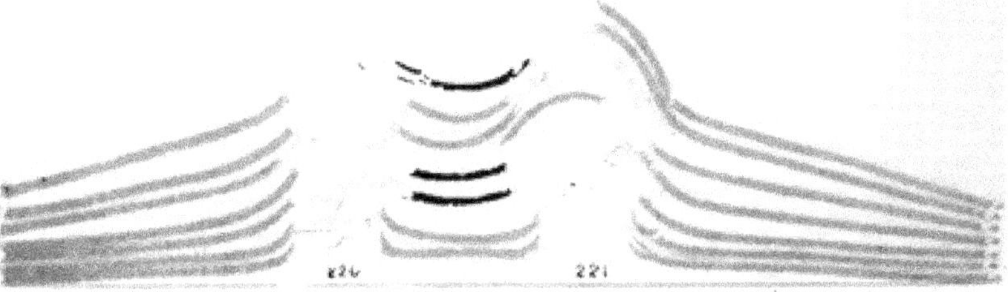

Section through A'B.' (See front view)

Scale of sections 6"=1' or ½ size.

Section through C'D'

TABLE XI.

No. of round.	Thickness of plate.	Weight of charge.	Form of shot. (*See Plate III.*)	Penetration, &c. (*Deepest point.*)
392	Six 1/8-in. plates in contact.	900 grains.	Cylindro-spherical.	5/8 inch.
391	Six 3/8-in. plates in contact.	900 grains.	Cylindrical.	1/2 inch.
398	Same separated 1-16 inch.	900 grains.	Cylindrical.	1 inch.
397	Same separated 1-16 inch.	900 grains.	Cylindro-spherical.	3/4 inch.
399	Same separated 1/8 inch.	900 grains.	Cylindro-spherical.	Clean hole.
393	Same separated 1/4 inch.	900 grains.	Cylindrical.	Clean hole.
400	Same separated 1/2 inch.	900 grains.	Cylindrical.	Clean hole.
395	Same separated 1/2 inch.	900 grains.	Cylindro-spherical.	Clean hole.
407	1/4 inch and 1/2 inch.	900 grains.	Cylindro-spherical.	5/8 inch and 1/4 inch. (See 403 and 404, Plate XII. chart.)
408	1/4 inch and 1/2 inch.	900 grains.	Cylindrical.	Same.
433	1 1/2 inch perforated with 3/4-inch holes.	900 grains.	Cylindrical.	Just through.
434	1 1/2 inch perforated with 3/4-inch holes.	900 grains.	Ogival, (long point.)	Through and 3 1/2 inches into an oak beam.
436	Same with holes 1 inch deep.	900 grains.	Ogival, (long point.)	1 1/4 inch.
437	Same with holes 1 inch deep.	900 grains.	Cylindrical.	3/4 inch.

[NOTE.] See "Separated Plates" and "Perforated Plates."

WROUGHT IRON.

(See following plate)

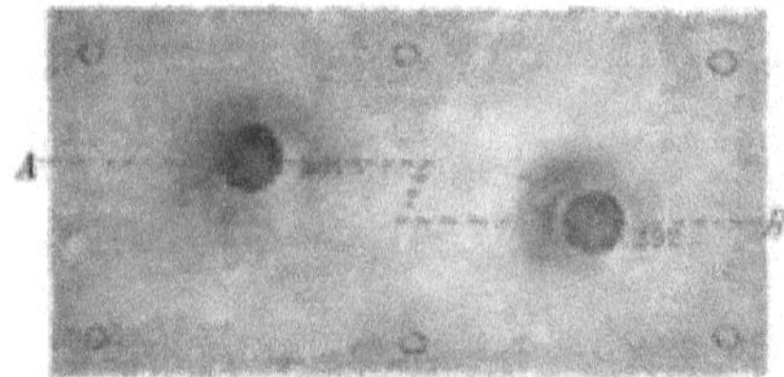

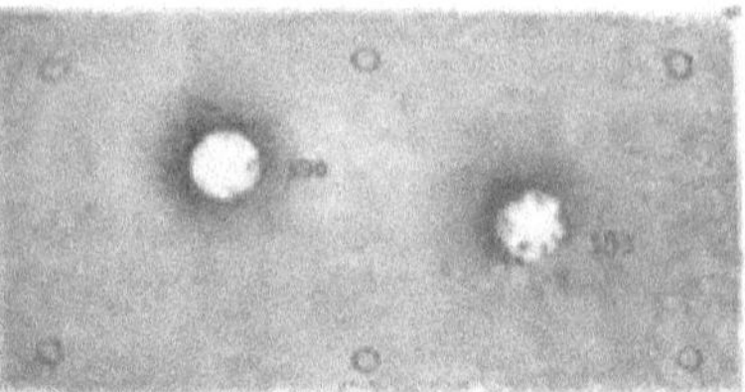

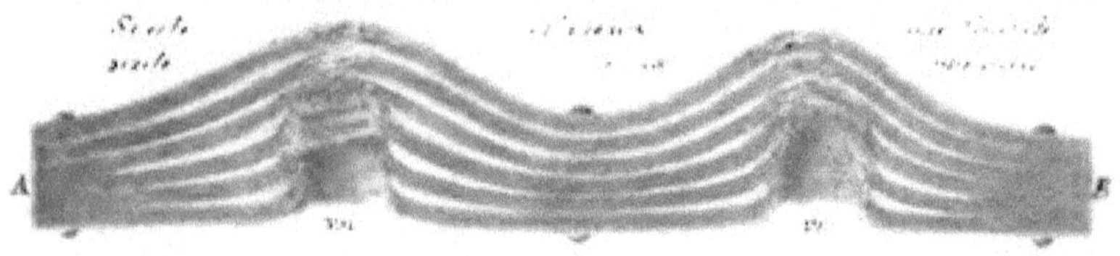

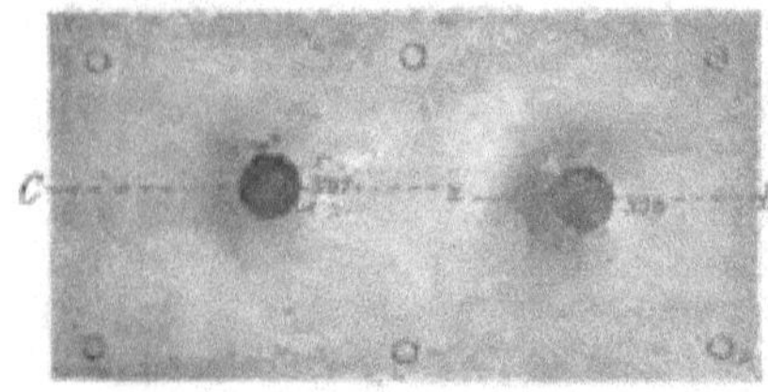

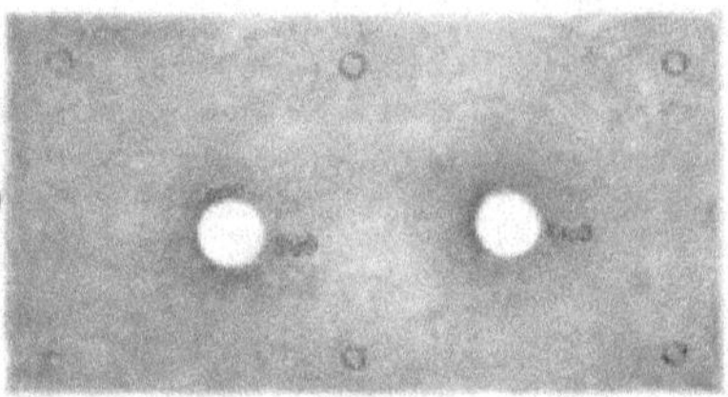

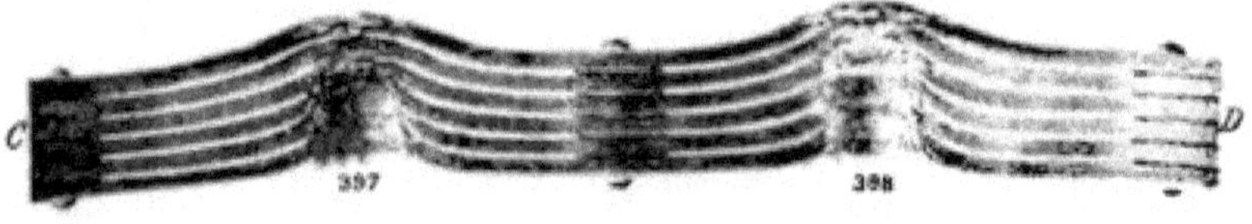

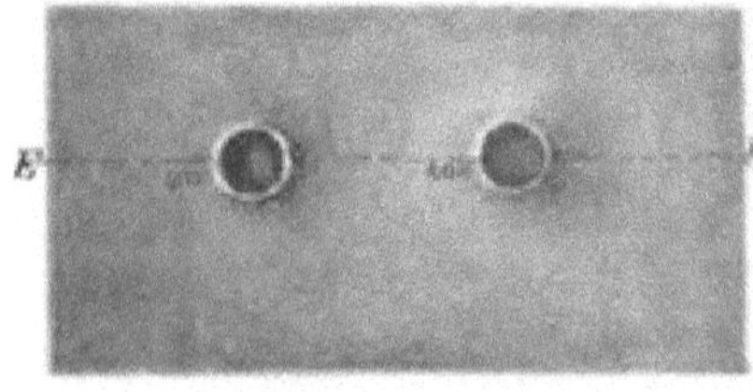

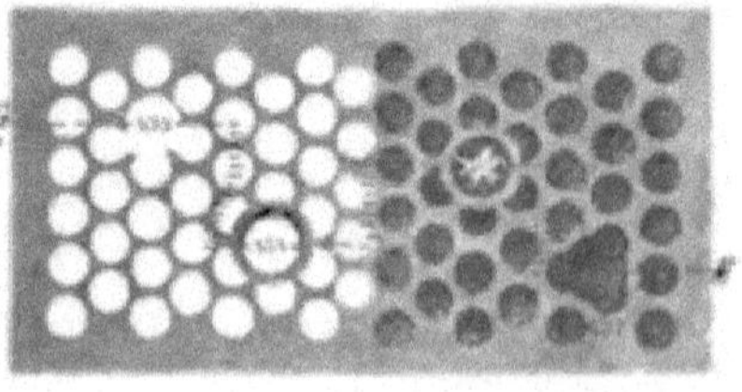

(See preceding plate)

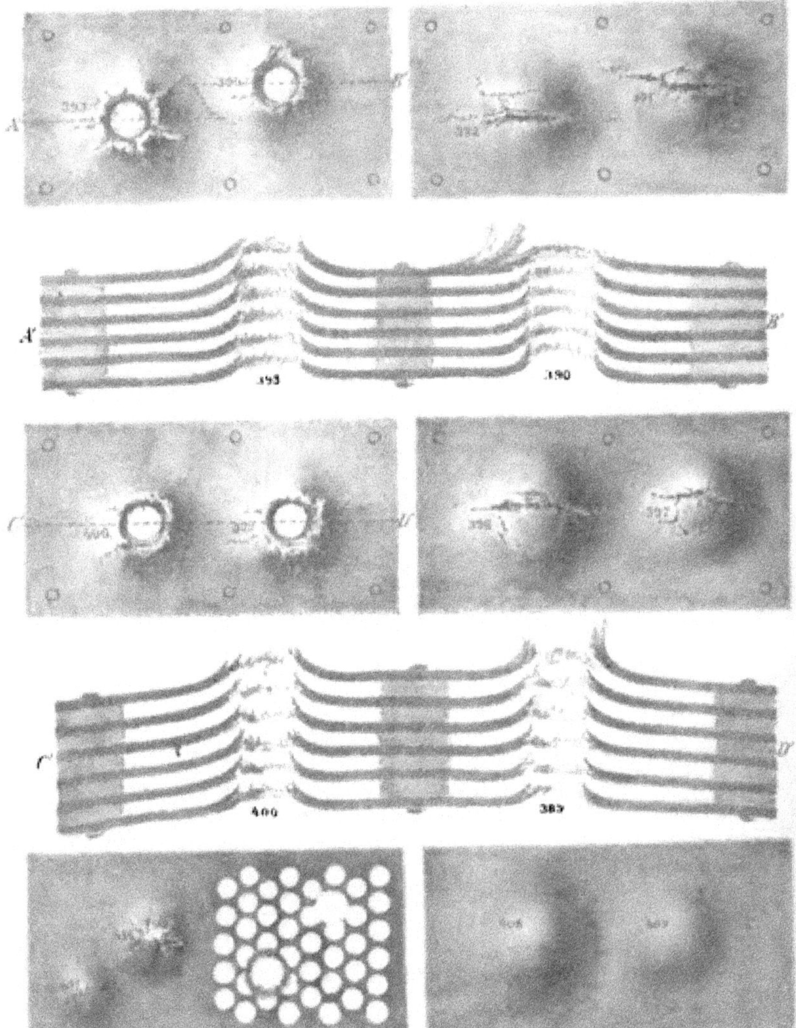

TABLE XII.

No. of round.	Thickness of plate.	Weight of charge.	Form of shot. (*See Plate III.*)	Penetration, &c. (*Deepest point.*)	
414	3 inches.	900 grains.	Cylindrical.	⅝ inch.	Puddled iron, partially hammered.
415	3 inches.	900 grains.	Ogival.	⅞ inch.	
421	3 inches.	900 grains.	Ogival.	1⅝ inch.	
416	3 inches.	900 grains.	Ogival.	1⅝ inch.	Puddled iron, compressed only with the rabble.
417	3 inches.	900 grains.	Cylindrical.	⅝ inch.	
420	3 inches.	900 grains.	Ogival.	Through, plate broken in two.	
418	3 inches.	900 grains.	Ogival.	3⅝ inches.	Lead and wire netting.
419	3 inches.	900 grains.	Cylindrical.	1⅝ inch.	
422	3 inches.	900 grains.	Ogival.	Clean hole.	
386	Two ⅝-inch plates with ⅝-in. sq're lead bars betw. them.	900 grains.	Cylindrical.	Through first plate and indented second.	
387		900 grains.	Ogival.	Through first plate and indented second.	
395	Tubular target.	900 grains.	Cylindrical.	Penetrated to rear plate.	
394	Tubular target.	900 grains.	Cylindro-spherical.	Through; struck joint in rear plate.	
396	Tubular target.	900 grains.	Cylindro-spherical.	Through; rear plate ripped off but not perforated by either of these shot.	

[NOTE.] See "Puddled Iron," "Tubular Target," and "Plates separated by bars of lead."

IRON, LEAD, ETC.

(see following plate)

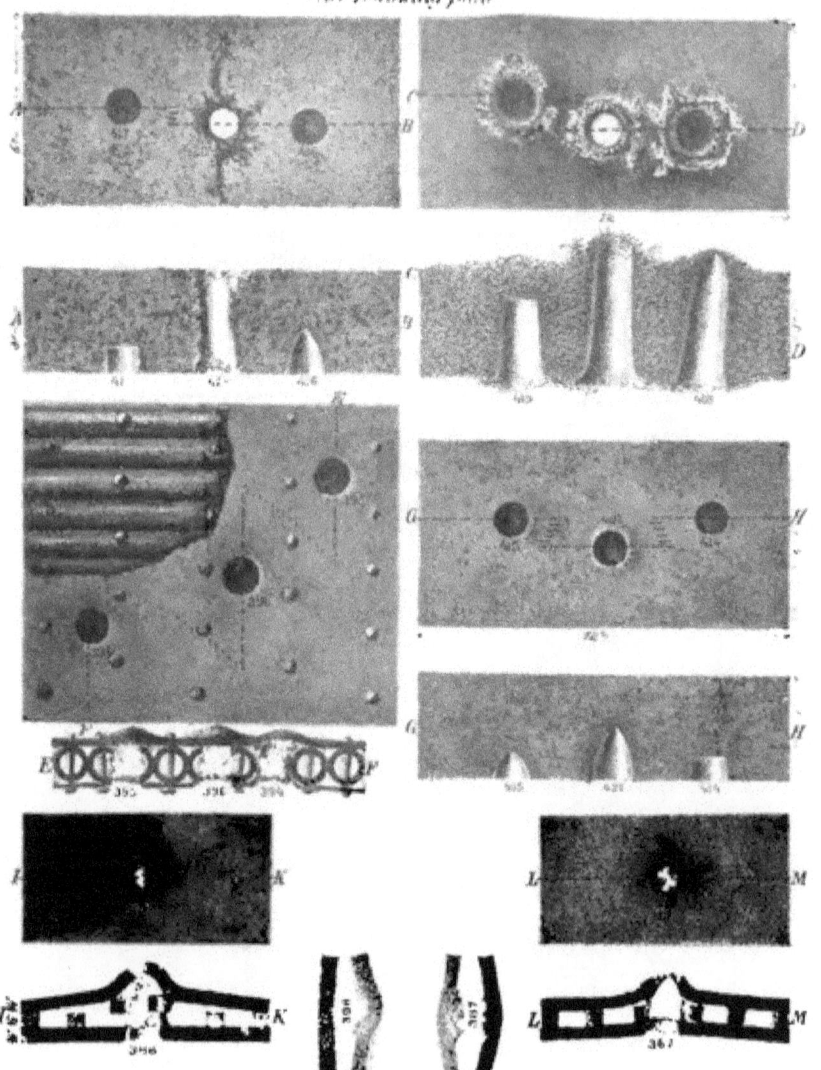

Scale ¼ or 3 to 1'

(See preceding plate)

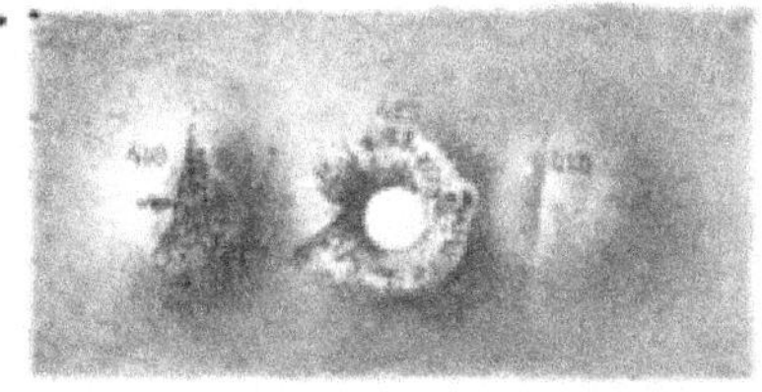

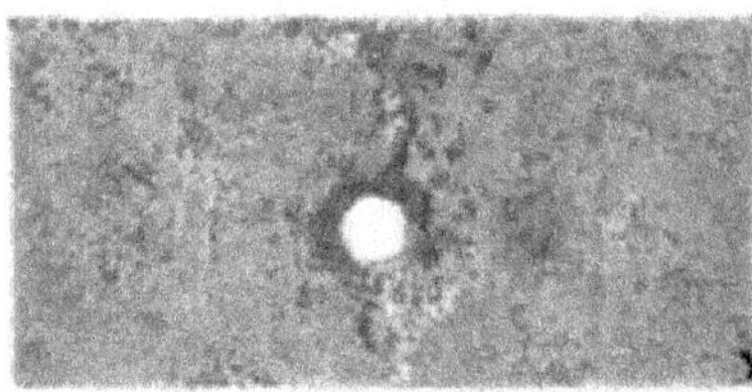

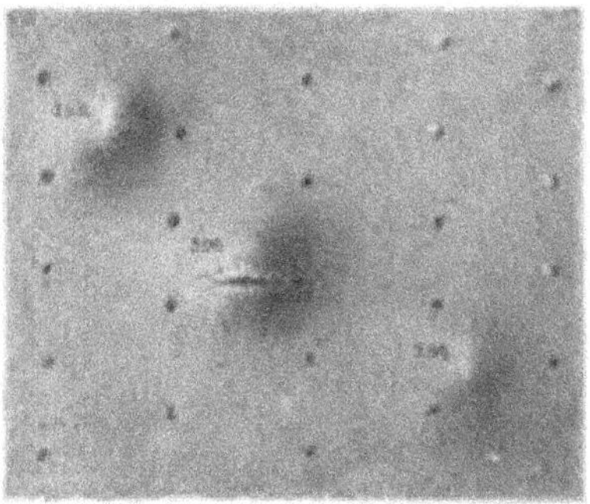

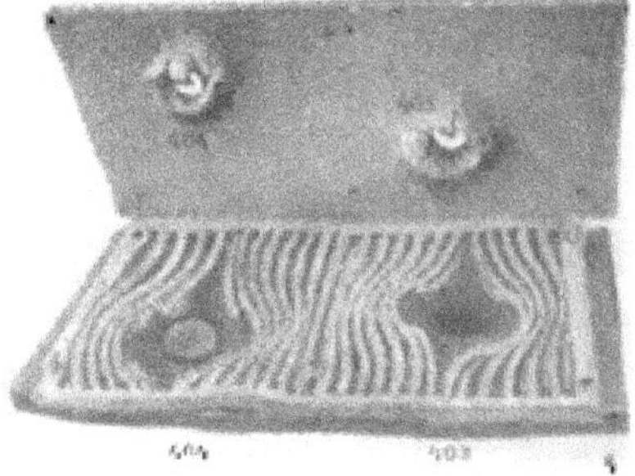

TABLE XIII.

No. of round.	Thickness of plate.	Weight of charge.	Form of shot. (*See Plate III.*)	Penetration, &c. (*Deepest point.*)
224	Girder target. Whole amount of iron equivalent to a ½-inch plate.	300 grains.	Spherical.	¾ inch. Backing not disturbed; no bolts broken.
225		300 grains.	Cylindrical.	1 inch. One beam and several bolts broken.
226		300 grains.	Cylindrical.	17-16 inch. Several bolts broken.
227		300 grains.	Ogival.	1½ inch. Shot stuck in target; point just touched first plate of backing.
228		300 grains.	Cylindrical.	⅝ inch. This shot struck where the lead had filled the spaces between the fragments of iron.
229		300 grains.	Ogival.	Effect similar to the 227th round; the shot turned, passing through the web of one of the beams, breaking it in two. None of these shot touched the wooden backing, and the plate against which the beams rested received only slight bends from the points of the shot.

[NOTE.] See "Girder Target."

PLATE XIII.

BEAM TARGET.

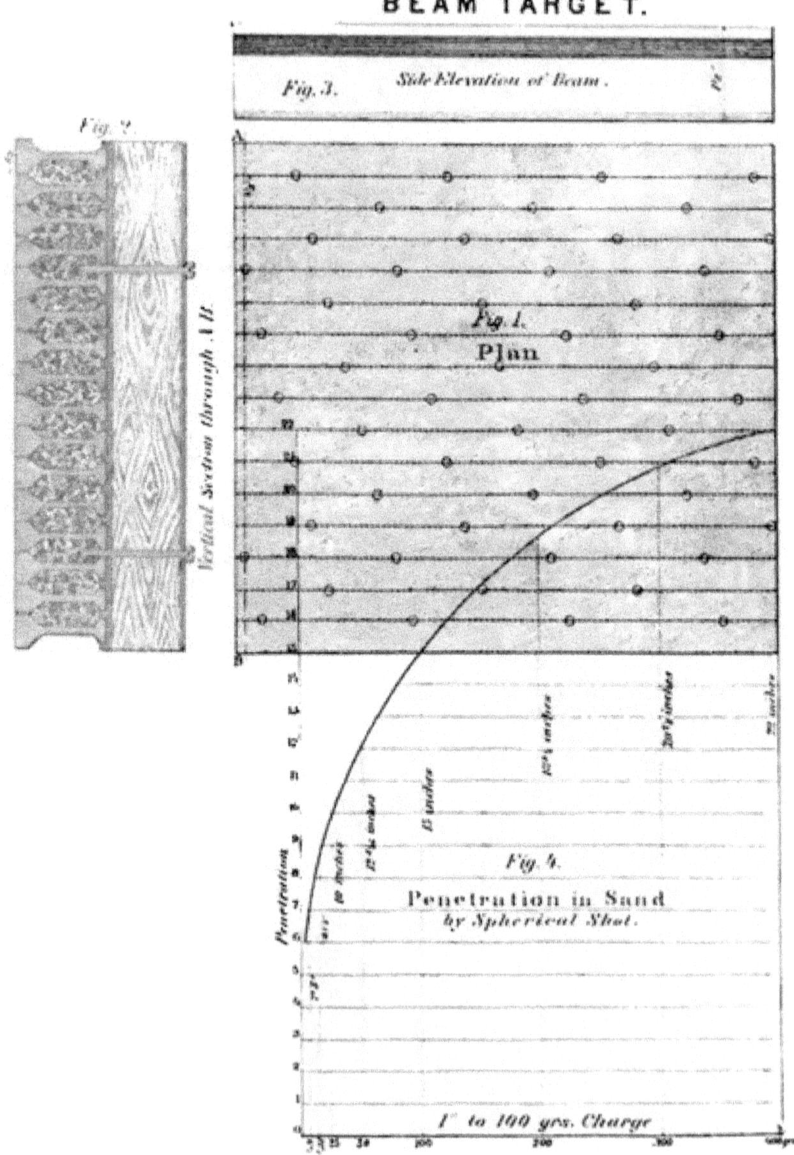

TABLE XIV.

No. of round.	Thickness of plate.	Weight of charge.	Form of shot. (*See Plate III.*)	Penetration, &c. (*Perfect point.*)
237[I]	[illegible] inch wrought, [illegible] in. chilled, [illegible] in. wrought.	[illegible] grains.	Ogival.	Through [illegible] inch plate. Chilled plate broken as shown in engraving.
237[II]	[illegible] inch wrought, 1 inch chilled, [illegible] in. wrought.	[illegible] grains.	Ogival.	Same result. Shot flattened at point.
237[III]	[illegible] inch wrought, 1½ in. chilled, [illegible] in. wrought.	[illegible] grains.	Ogival.	Same result. Shot flattened at point.
237[IV]	[illegible] inch wrought, 2 in. chilled, [illegible] in. wrought.	[illegible] grains.	Ogival.	Same result. Shot somewhat upset, but penetrated chilled plate slightly.
237[V]	[illegible] inch wrought, 2 in. chilled, [illegible] in. wrought.	[illegible] grains.	Ogival.	Chilled plate cracked in three pieces. Shot penetrated [illegible] plate, and [illegible] inch into chilled plate.

[Note.] See "Chilled Iron."

PLATE XIV.

CHILLED IRON.

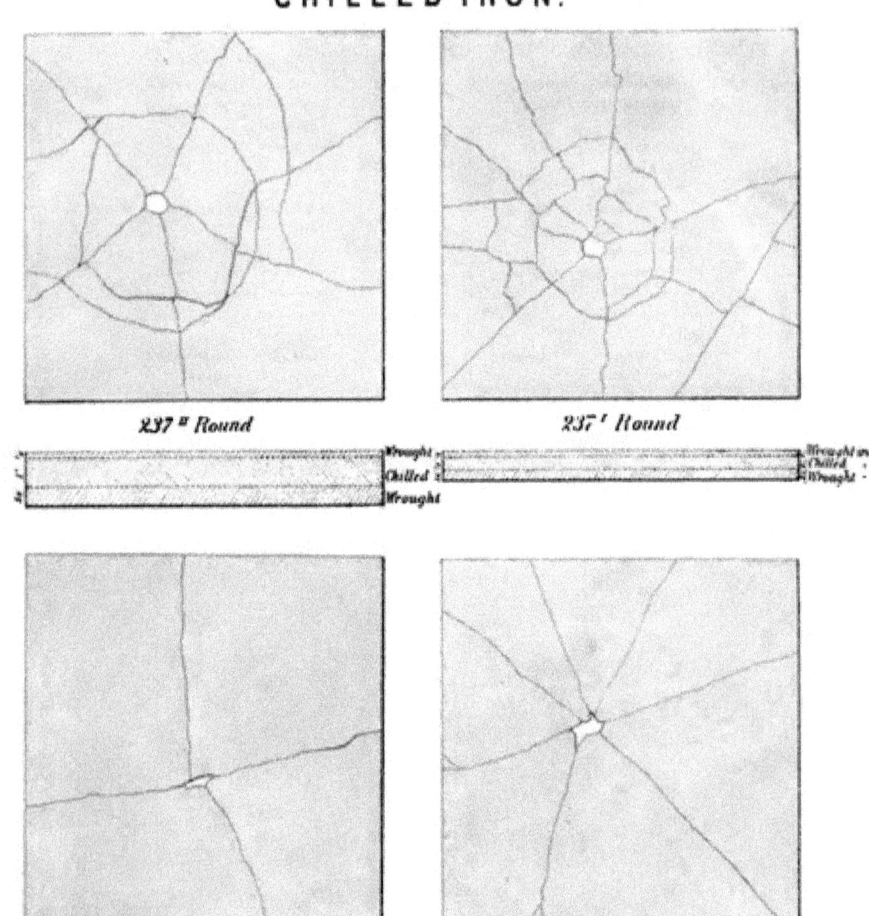

237 II Round

237 I Round

237 IV Round

237 III Round

TABLE XV.

No. of round.	Thickness of plate.	Weight of charge.	Form of shot. (*See Plate III.*)	Penetration, &c. (*Deepest point.*)
250	½ inch Bessemer steel, (cast.)	300 grains.	Spherical.	Hardest quality of steel.
251		300 grains.	Spherical.	Hardest quality of steel.
252		300 grains.	Spherical.	Hardest quality of steel.
254		300 grains.	Spherical.	Through. Softest quality.
255		300 grains.	Spherical.	Through. Softest quality.
266		300 grains.	Spherical.	⅜ inch. Medium.
267		300 grains.	Spherical.	⅜ inch. Medium.
291		300 grains.	Spherical.	⅜ inch. Medium.

[NOTE.] See "Bessemer Steel."

BESSEMER STEEL.

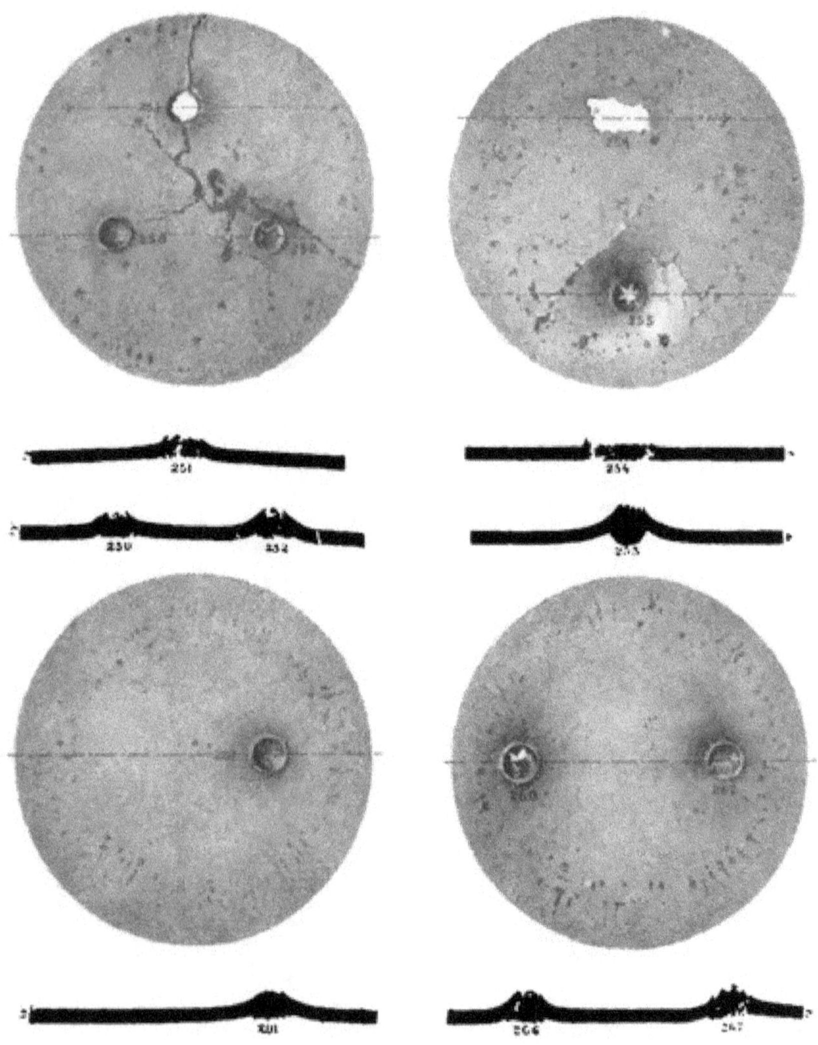

Scale 3" = 1'.

TABLE XVI.

No. of round.	Thickness of plate.	Weight of charge.	Form of shot. (*See Plate III.*)	Penetration, &c. (*Deepest point.*)
245	1 inch.	300 grains.	Spherical.	½ inch. Medium quality of steel.
246	1 inch.	300 grains.	Cylindro-spherical.	⅝ inch. Medium quality of steel.
247	1 inch.	300 grains.	Cylindrical.	⅜ inch. Medium quality of steel.
259	1 inch.	300 grains	Cylindrical.	3-16 inch. Shot broke. Hardest quality.
260	1 inch.	300 grains.	Ogival.	9-16 inch. Hardest quality.
268	1 inch.	300 grains.	Cylindro-spherical.	⅜ inch. Softest quality.
269	1 inch.	300 grains.	Cylindrical.	⅝ inch. Softest quality.
293	⅝ inch.	300 grains.	Spherical.	3-16 inch. Hardest quality.

[NOTE.] See "Bessemer Steel."

BESSEMER STEEL.

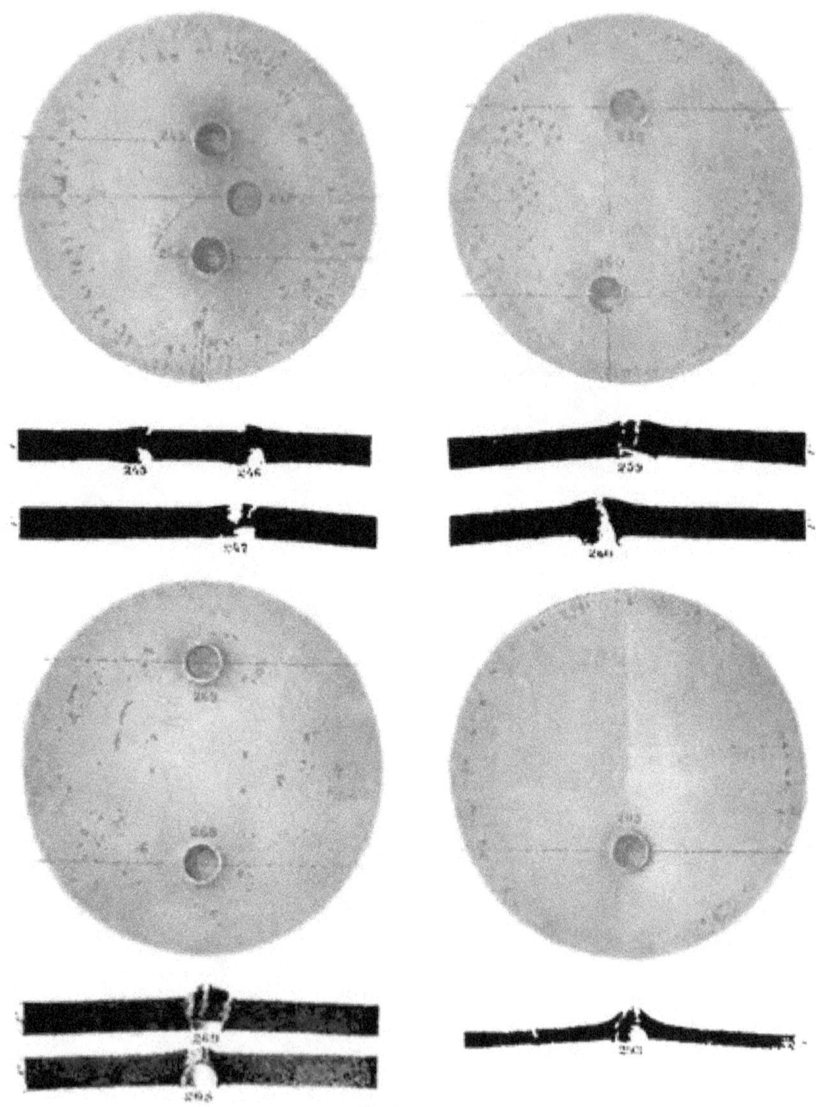

Scale 3 - 1.

TABLE XVII.

No. of round.	Thickness of plate.	Weight of charge.	Form of shot. (*See Plate III.*)	Penetration, &c. (*Deepest point.*)
[illegible]	[illegible]-inch wrought iron.	300 grains.	Cylindro-spherical.	[illegible] inch.
[illegible]	[illegible]-inch Bessemer steel, and 3 inches lead concrete.	300 grains.	Cylindrical.	[illegible] inch.
302 (Back of plate.)	Same target.	300 grains.	Cylindro-spherical.	3 inches.
307	Same target.	500 grains.	Cylindrical.	
308	Same target.	500 grains.	Ogival, (long.)	
330	[illegible]-inch iron & 1[illegible]-inch lead concrete.	300 grains.	Cylindro-spherical.	[illegible] inch.
331	Same target.	300 grains.	Cylindrical.	[illegible] inch.
332 (Back of plate.)	Same target.	300 grains.	Cylindro-spherical.	2[illegible] inches.
333	Same target.	300 grains.	Cylindrical.	Clean hole.
316	Two [illegible]-inch plates, with 1[illegible] inch of lead concrete between. Front plate steel, rear one iron.	300 grains.	Cylindro-spherical.	2 inches.
318	Two [illegible]-inch plates, with 1[illegible] inch of lead concrete between. Front plate steel, rear one iron.	300 grains.	Cylindrical.	1[illegible] inches.
347	Four [illegible]-inch iron plates, with three [illegible]-inch layers of lead concrete.	300 grains.	Cylindro-spherical.	1[illegible] inches.
[illegible]	Four [illegible]-inch iron plates, with three [illegible]-inch layers of lead concrete.	300 grains.	Cylindrical.	1[illegible] inches.

[Note.] See "Lead Concrete."

IRON AND LEAD CONCRETE.

(See following plate.)

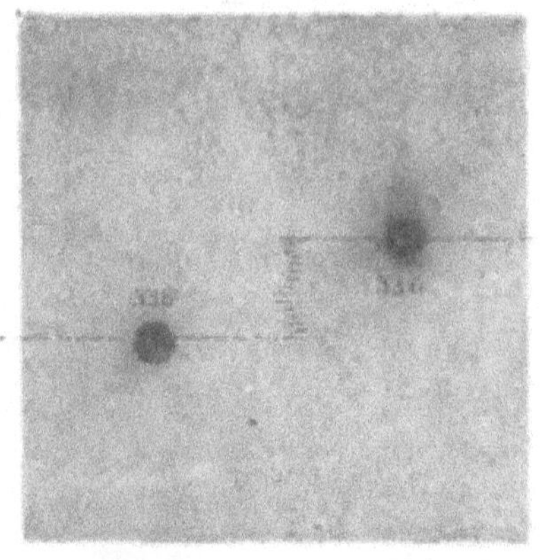

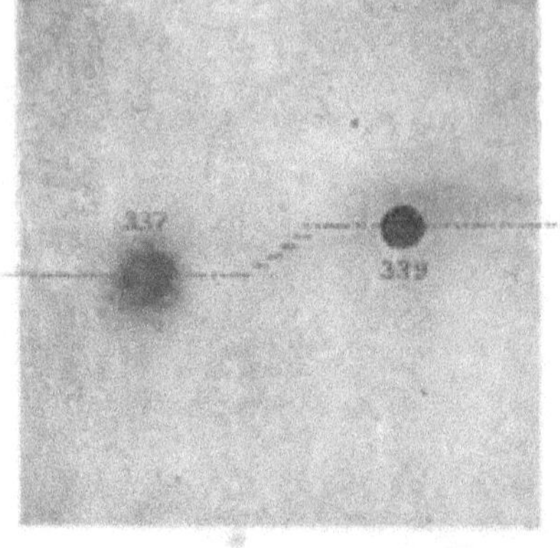

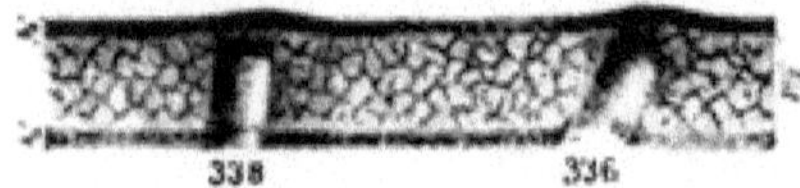

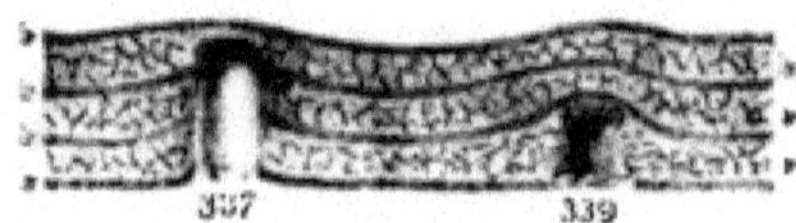

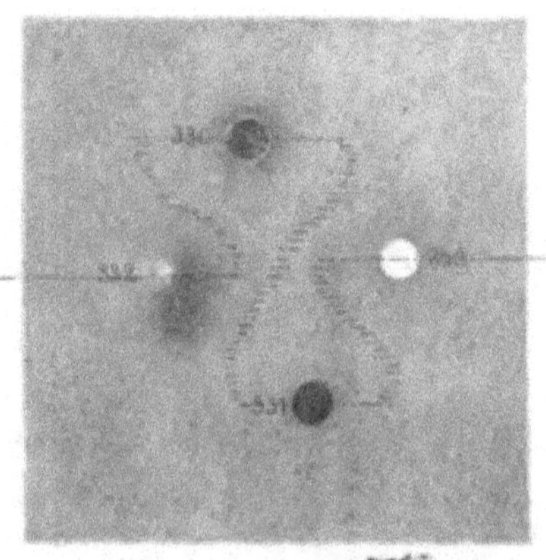

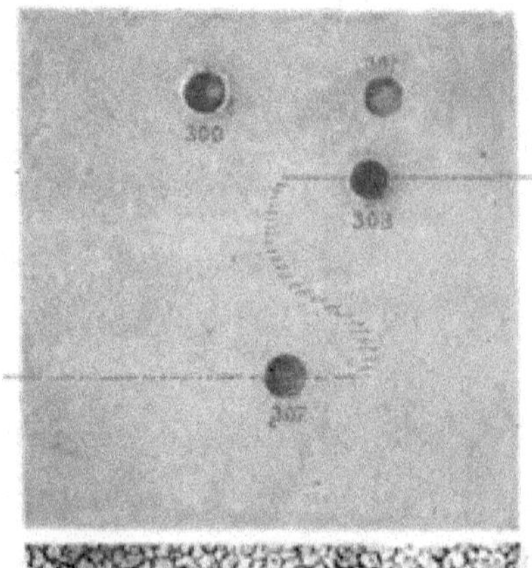

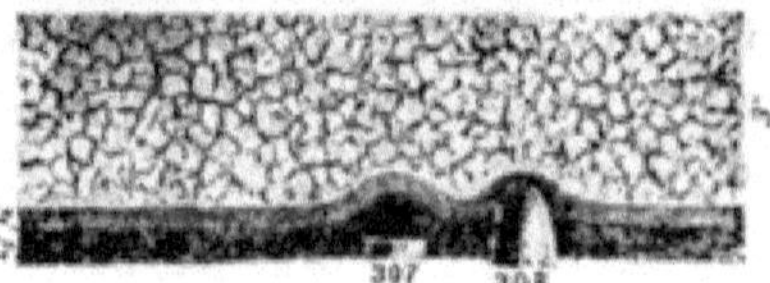

(See preceding plate)

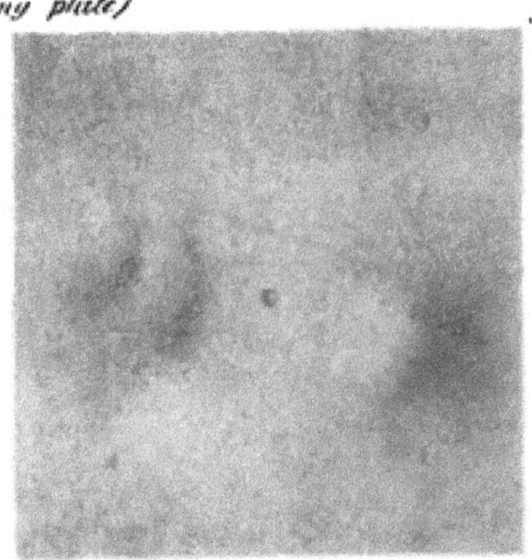

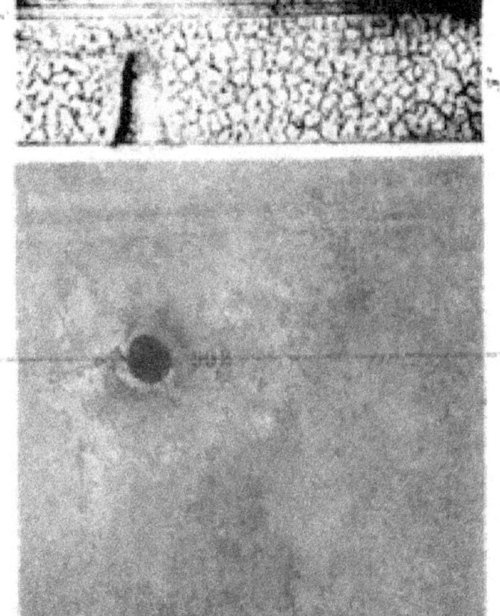

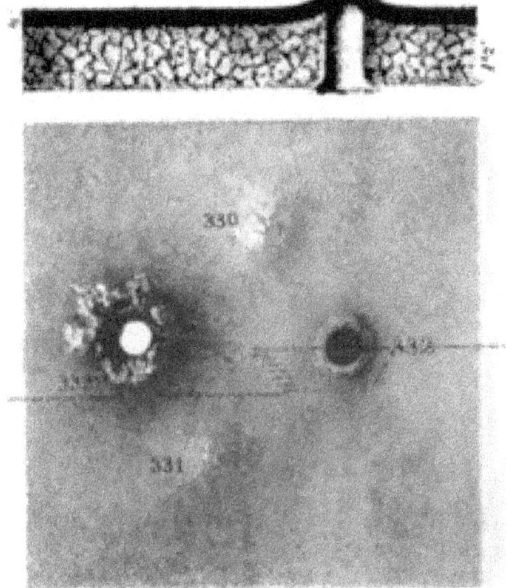

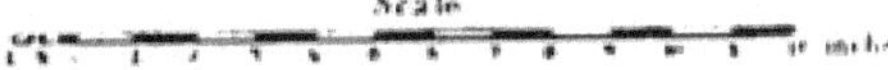

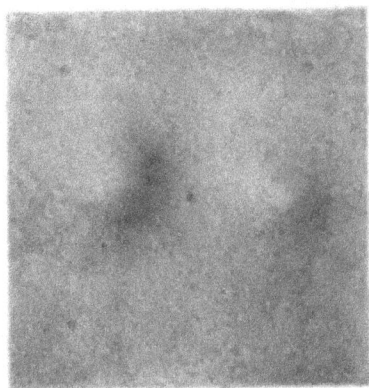

TABLE XVIII.

No. of round.	Thickness of plate.	Weight of charge.*	Form of shot.	Penetration, &c.
327	⅝-inch Bessemer steel, backed by 3 inches of lead concrete.	900 grains.	Cylindrical.	1⅞ inches.
328	⅝-inch Bessemer steel, backed by 3 inches of lead concrete.	900 grains.	Cylindrical.	⅜ inch. Shot upset.
329	⅝-inch Bessemer steel, backed by 3 inches of lead concrete.	900 grains.	Cylindro-spherical.	1¼ inches.
334	4 inches of soft lead.	900 grains.	Cylindro-spherical.	Through.
335	4 inches of soft lead.	900 grains.	Cylindrical.	2⅝ inches.
325	⅝ inch.	900 grains.	Cylindro-spherical.	⅝ inch.
326	1 inch.	900 grains.	Cylindro-spherical.	
47	⅝ inch.	900 grains.	Cylindrical.	Through.
370	1⅝ inch composition, (gun metal.)	900 grains.	Cylindrical.	⅜ inch.
371	1⅝ inch composition, (gun metal.)	900 grains.	Ogival, (long.)	1⅝ inches.
372	1⅝ inch composition, (gun metal.)	900 grains.	Cylindrical.	Just through.

[Note.] * See "Lead Concrete," &c.

IRON, LEAD & GUN METAL.

(See following plate)

LEAD

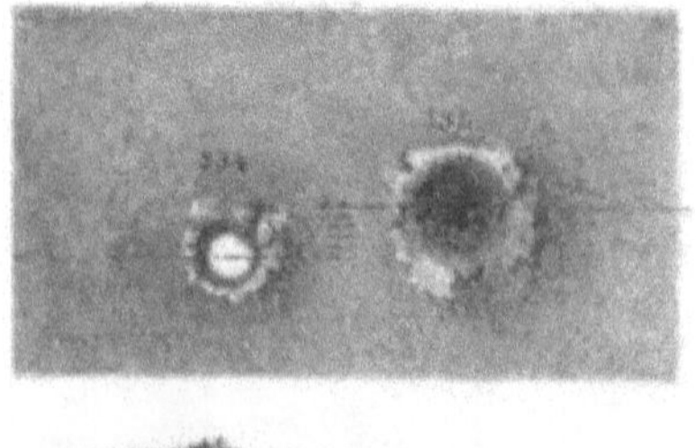

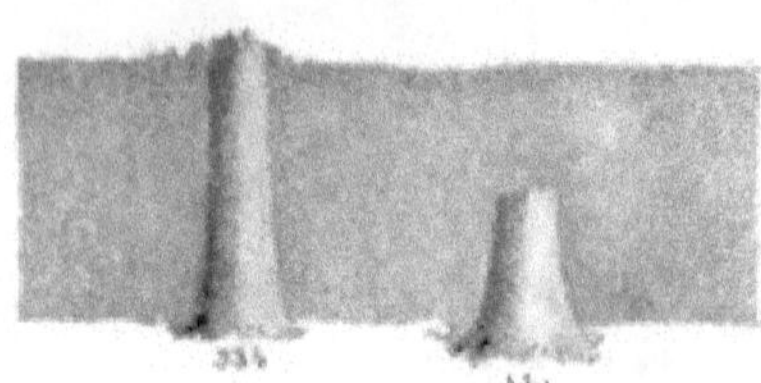

WROUGHT IRON

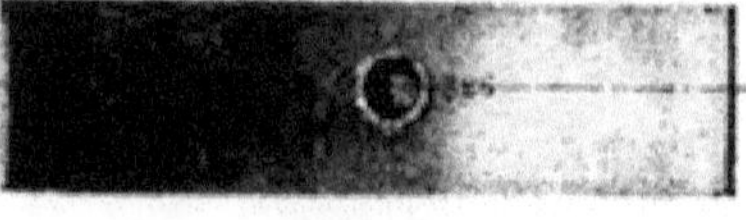

WROUGHT IRON

LEAD CONCRETE

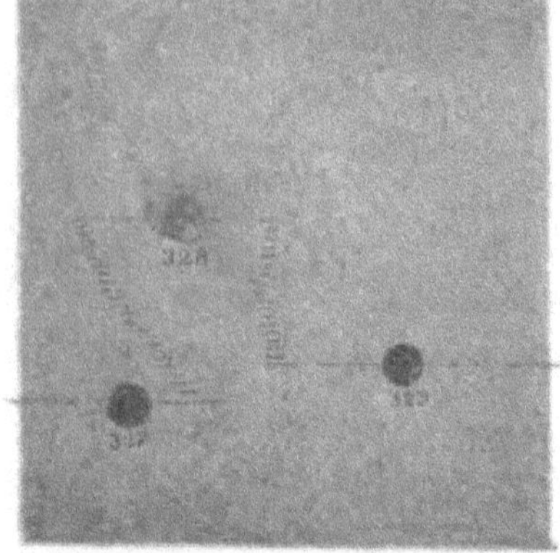

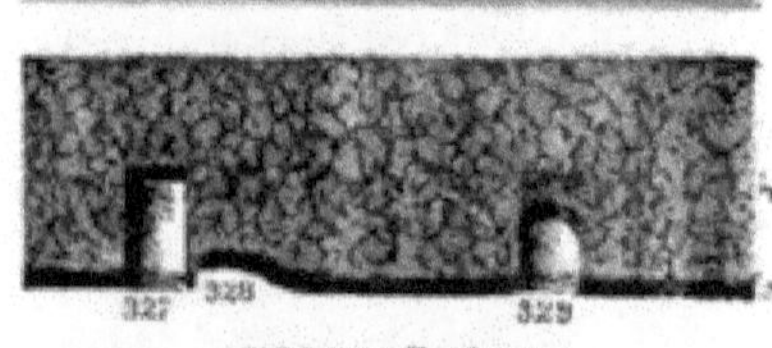

WROUGHT-IRON

GUN METAL

(See preceding plate)

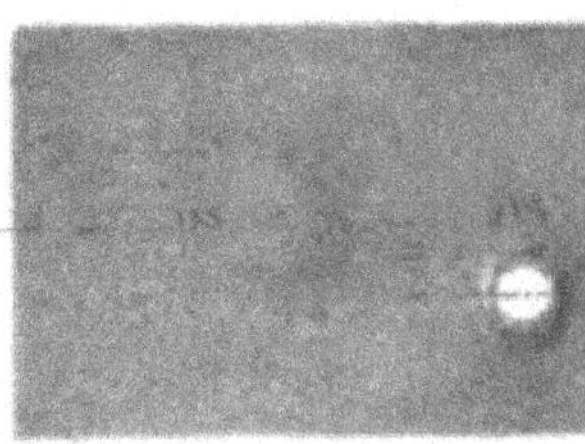

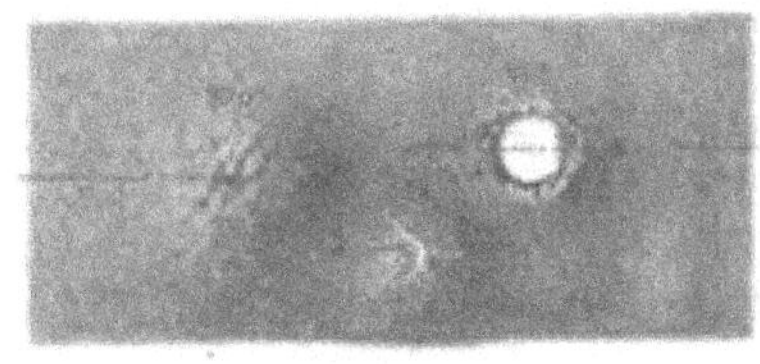

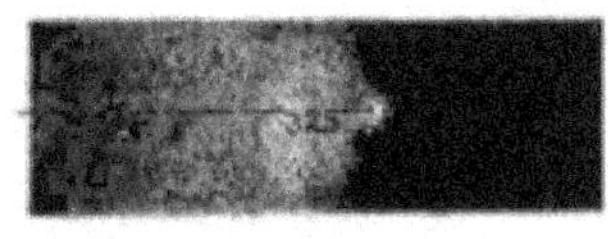

TABLE XIX.

No. of round.	Thickness of plate.	Weight of charge.	Form of shot.	Angle of incidence.	Penetration, &c.
452	3/8 inch.	300 grains.	Spherical.	45	Through.
453	1/4 inch.	300 grains.	Spherical.	45	Through.
454	3/4 inch.	300 grains.	Spherical.	45	Through.
455	5/8 inch.	300 grains.	Cylindrical.	45	Through.
456	1/4 inch.	300 grains.	Ogival.	45	Through.
457	5/8 inch.	300 grains.	Cylindrical.	60°	Through.
462	Four 1/8-inch plates riveted together.	300 grains.	Cylindrical.	45	Through.
463	Four 1/8-inch plates riveted together.	300 grains.	Ogival, (long.)	45	Through.
464	3/8 inch, backed with 1 3/4 inch of hickory.	300 grains.	Cylindrical.	80	Hole through plate and backing.
465	3/8 inch, backed with 1 7/8 inch of hickory.	300 grains.	Spherical.	80	Slight furrow in plate; backing not disturbed.

[NOTE.] See "Oblique Impact."

OBLIQUE IMPACT.

Scale ½ size.

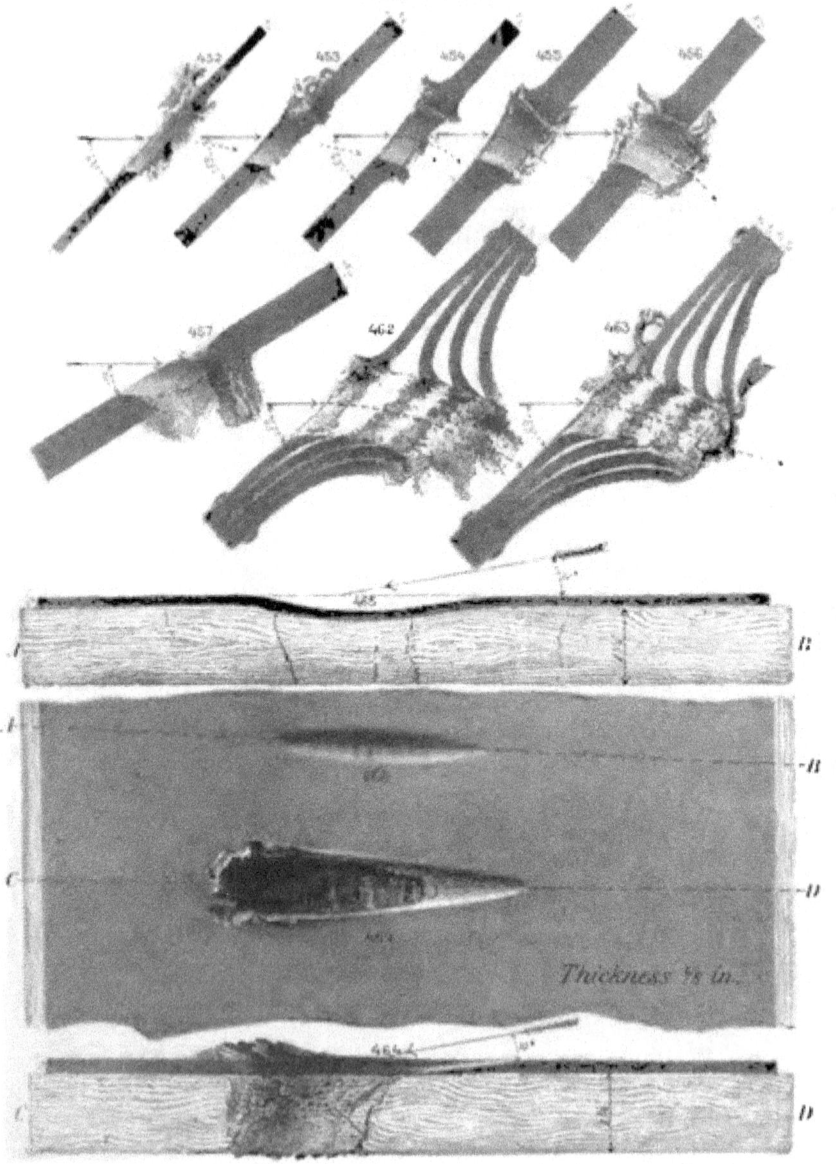

TABLE XX.

No. of round.	Thickness of plate.	Weight of charge.	Form of shot.	Angle of incidence.	Penetration, &c.
466	¼-inch, backed with 1¾ inch of hickory.	300 grains.	Cylindrical.	80°	Through plate.
467	½-inch, backed with 1¾ inch of hickory.	300 grains.	Ogival.	80	Slight furrow in plate.
468	½-inch, backed with 1¾ inch of hickory.	300 grains.	Spherical.	80	Indent slightly deeper.
469	⅜-inch, backed with 1¾ inch of hickory.	300 grains.	Cylindrical.	82	Hole through plate.
470	¼-inch, same backing.	300 grains.	Cylindrical.	84	Hole through plate.
471	¼-inch, same backing.	300 grains.	Cylindrical.	84	Hole larger than before.
473	⅜-inch, same backing.	300 grains.	Cylindrical.	87	Shot bit into plate & scooped out a groove ⅜-inch deep and 4 inches long.
474	⅜-inch, backed with 1¾ inch of hickory.	300 grains.	Cylindrical.	87	Hole through plate.

NOTE. See "Oblique Impact."

OBLIQUE IMPACT.

Scale ½ size.

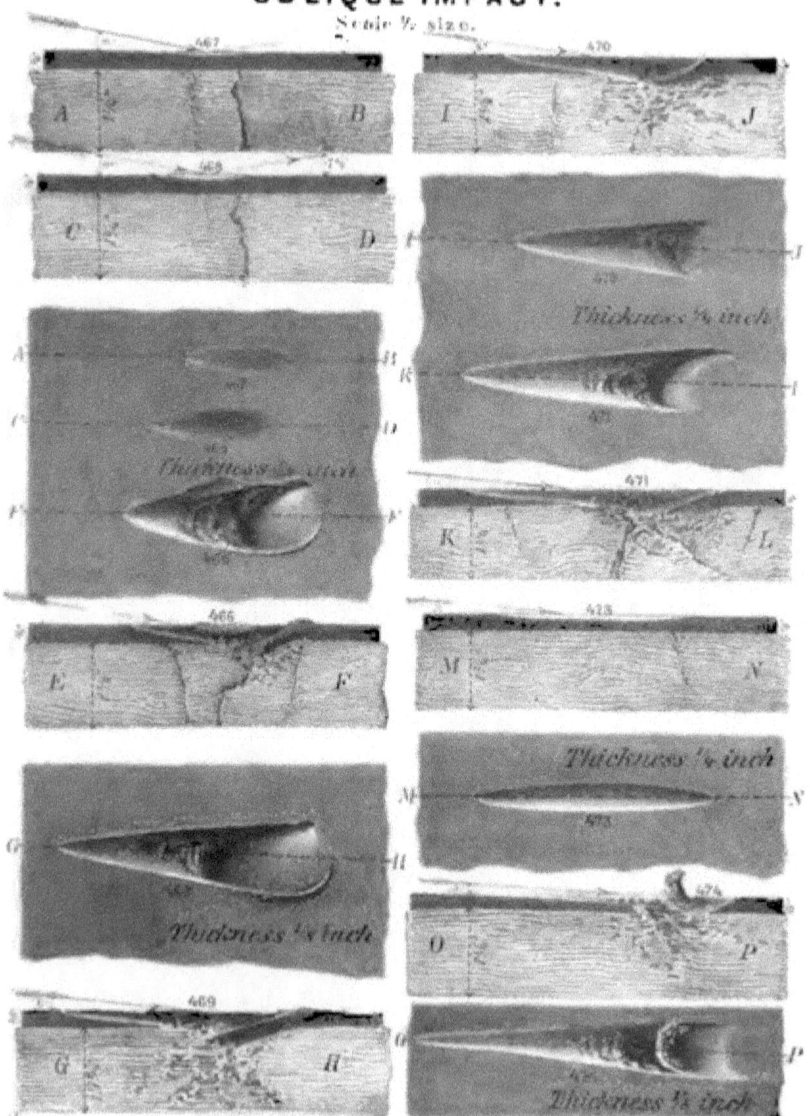

DIRECT AND OBLIQUE IMPACT.

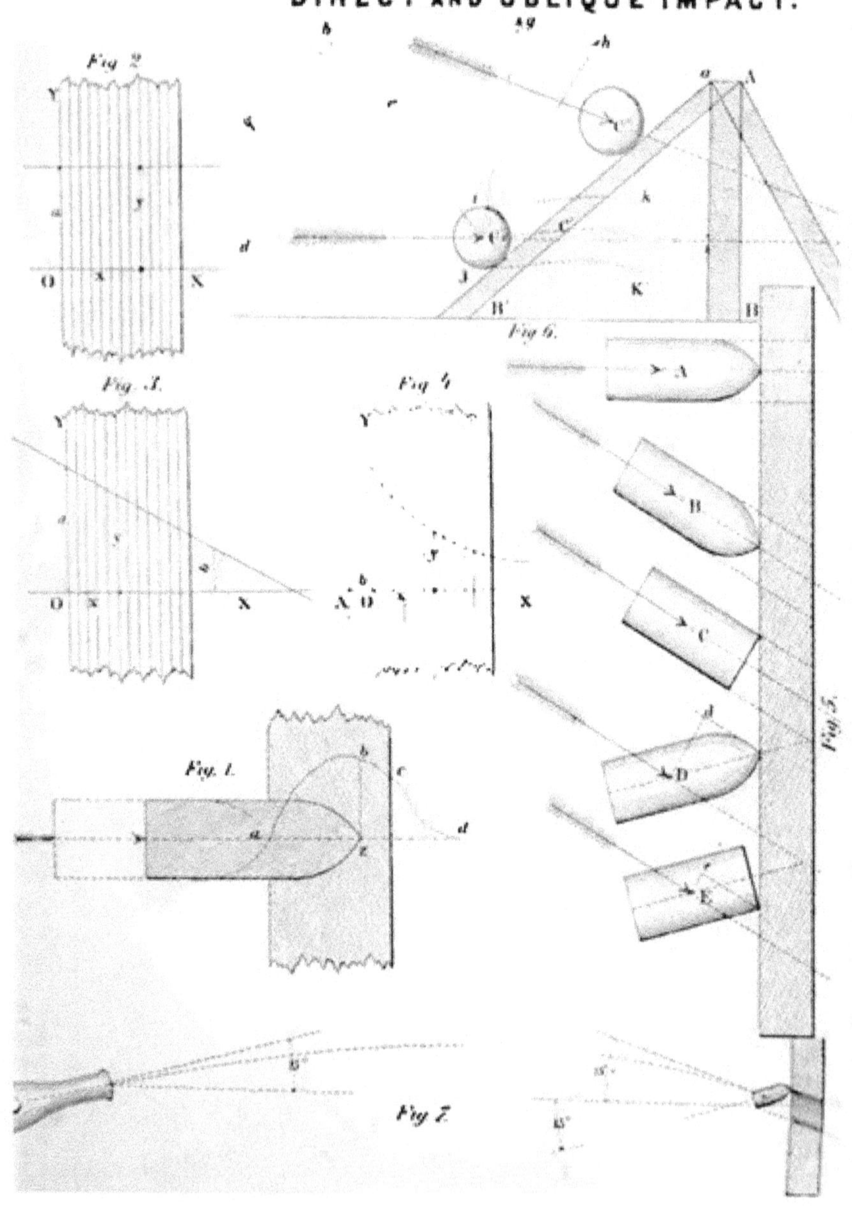

PLATE XXII.

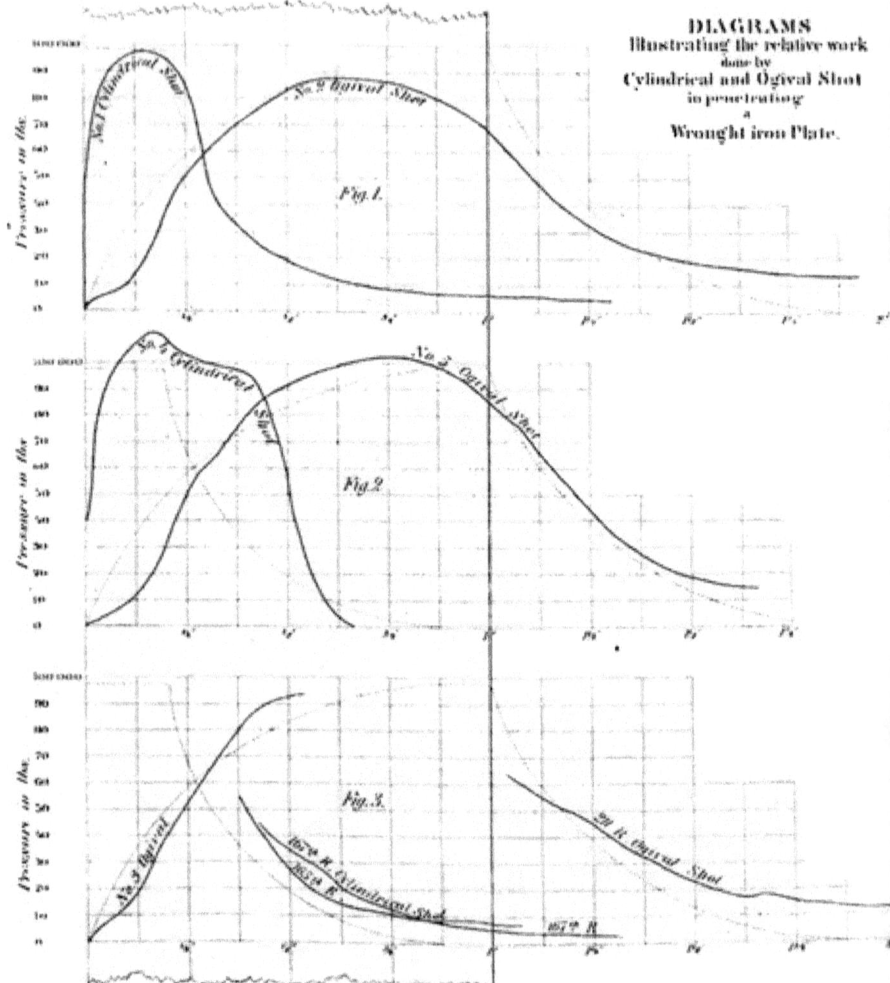
DIAGRAMS
Illustrating the relative work
done by
Cylindrical and Ogival Shot
in penetrating
a
Wrought iron Plate.
No. 1 Cylindrical Shot
No. 2 Ogival Shot
Fig. 1.
Fig. 2
Fig. 3.
Pressure in lbs.
Penetration in Inches.

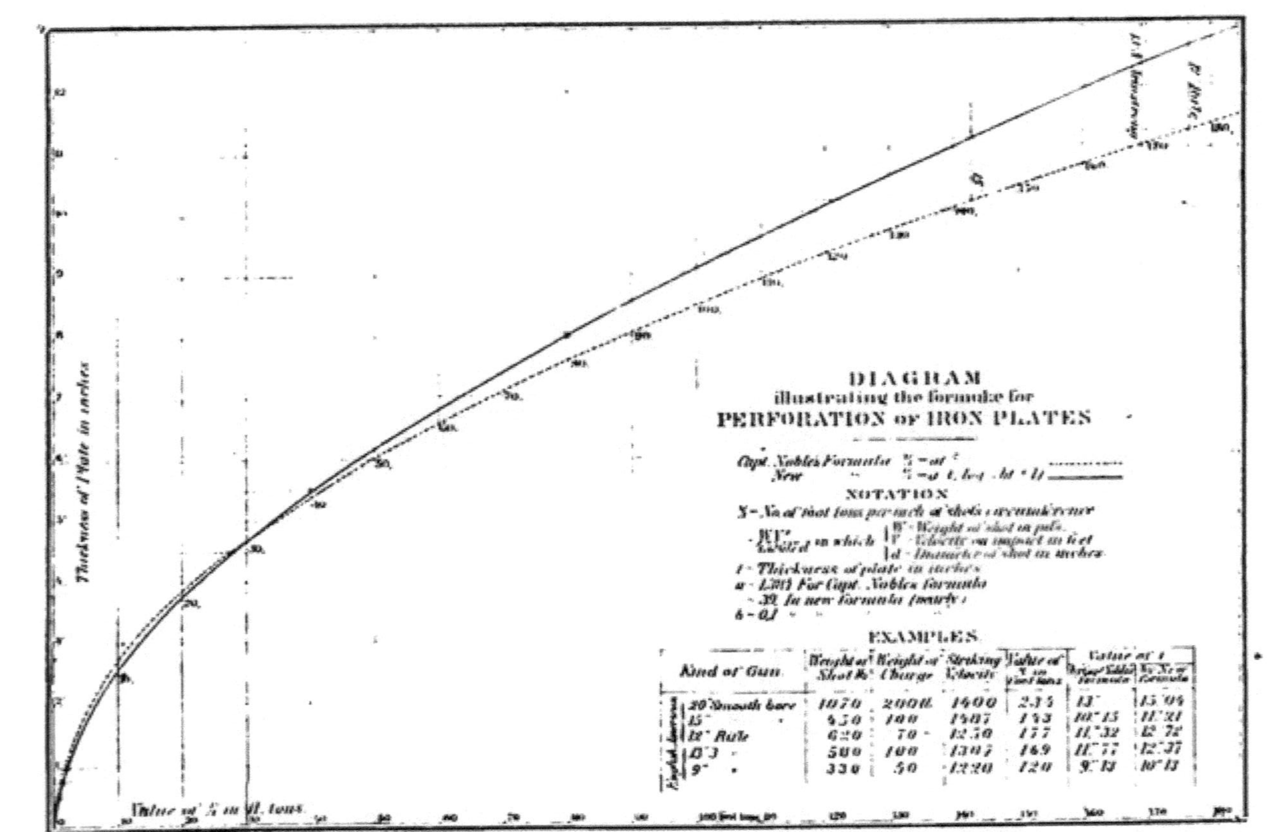

Kind of Gun	Weight of Shot lbs.	Weight of Charge	Striking Velocity	Value of N in foot tons	Value of t by Capt. Noble's formula	Value of t by New formula
20" Smooth bore	1070	200 lb.	1400	235	13"	15".04
15"	450	100	1507	153	10".15	11".31
12" Rifle	620	70	1250	177	11".32	12".72
13".3	500	100	1307	169	11".77	12".37
9"	330	50	1320	120	9".13	10".13

PLATE XXIV.

MISCELLANEOUS.

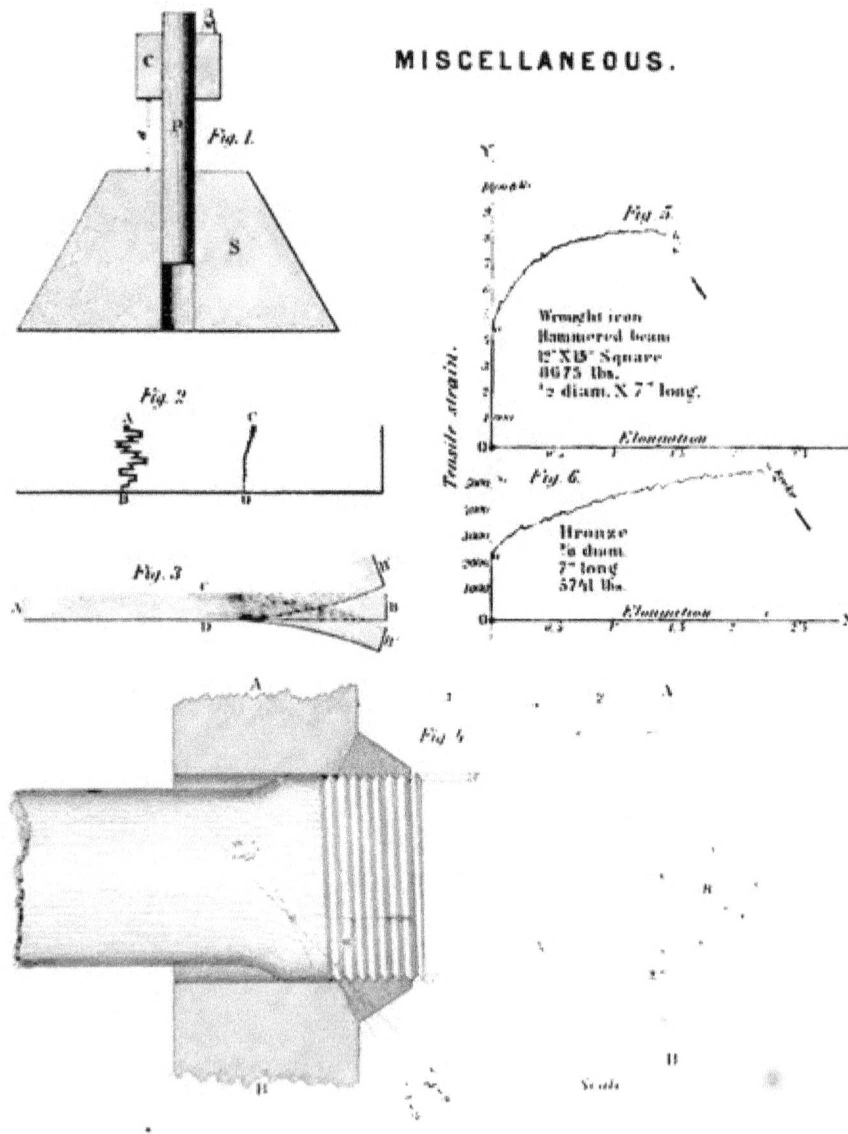

BOLTS.

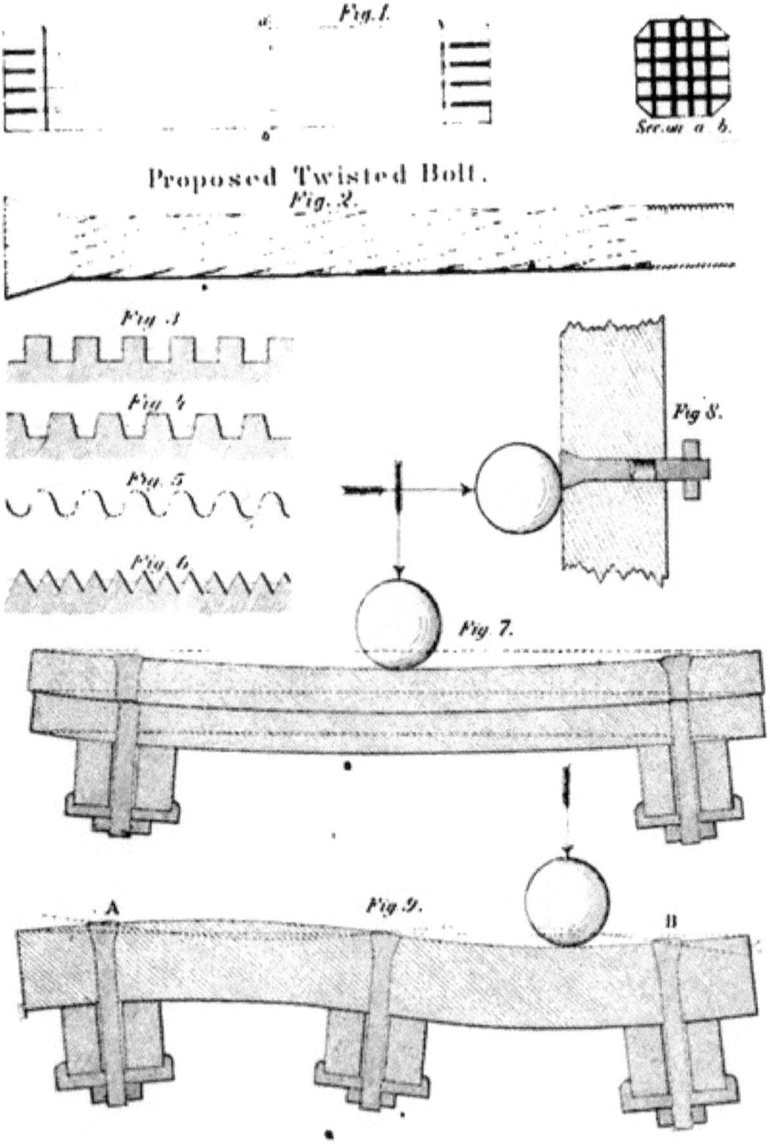

Fig. 1.

Proposed Twisted Bolt.

Fig. 2.

Fig. 3

Fig. 4

Fig. 5

Fig. 6

Fig. 7.

Fig. 8.

Fig. 9.

A

B

BOLTS.

Scale 2" = 1' or 1/6.

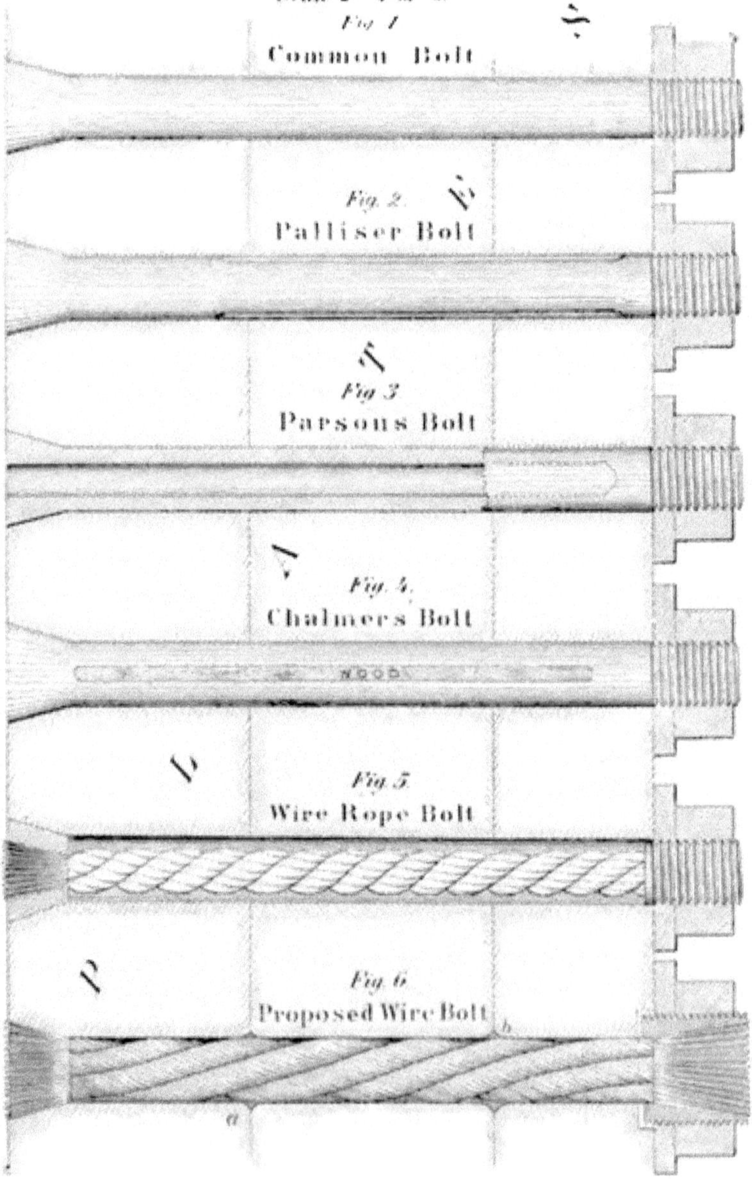

Fig. 1.
Common Bolt

Fig. 2.
Palliser Bolt

Fig. 3.
Parsons Bolt

Fig. 4.
Chalmers Bolt

WOOD

Fig. 5.
Wire Rope Bolt

Fig. 6.
Proposed Wire Bolt

b

a

MISCELLANEOUS.

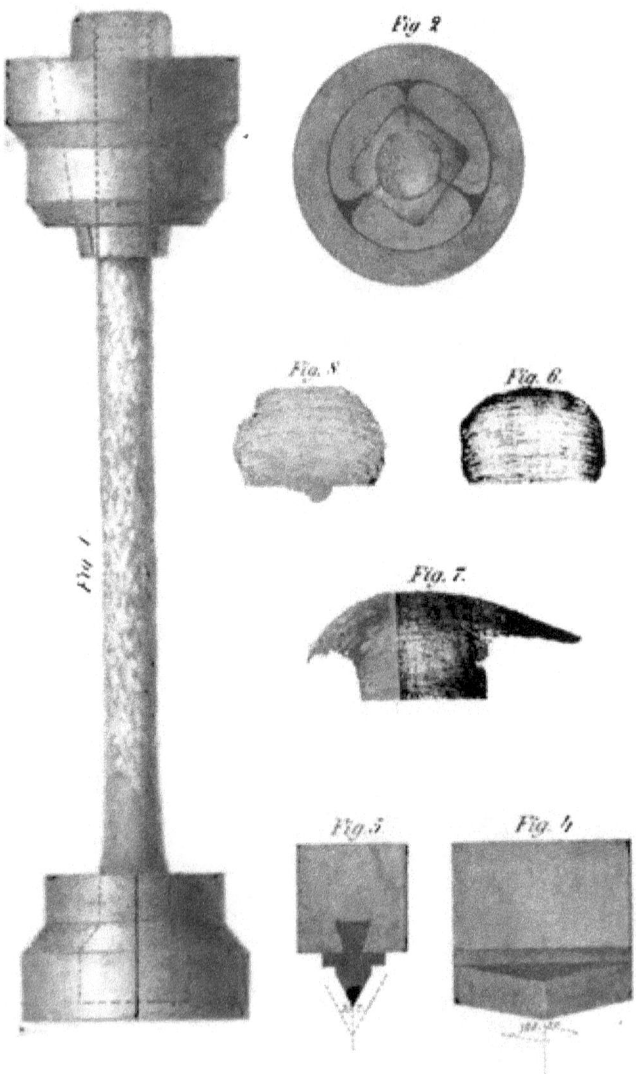

www.ingramcontent.com/pod-product-compliance
Lightning Source LLC
Chambersburg PA
CBHW030836270326
41928CB00007B/1087
* 9 7 8 3 7 4 2 8 6 2 5 6 3 *